the FAITH *we* PROFESS

D1019221

the FAITH

we PROFESS

A Catholic Guide
to the Apostles' Creed

PETER J. VAGHI

foreword by
Archbishop Donald W. Wuerl

ave maria press AMP notre dame, indiana

© 2008 by Peter J. Vaghi

Founded in 1865, Ave Maria Press is a ministry of the Indiana Province of Holy
Cross.

www.avemariapress.com

ISBN-10 1-59471-177-1 ISBN-13 978-1-59471-177-0

Cover and text design by David R. Scholtes.
Printed and bound in the United States of America.

Library of Congress Cataloging-in-Publication Data
Vaghi, Peter J.
  The faith we profess : a Catholic guide to the Apostles' Creed / Peter J. Vaghi.
    p. cm.
  Includes bibliographical references.
  ISBN-13: 978-1-59471-177-0 (pbk.)
  ISBN-10: 1-59471-177-1 (pbk.)
  1. Apostles' Creed 2. Catholic Church--Doctrines. I. Title.

BT993.3.V34 2008
238'.11--dc22
                            2008013081

Dedicated in memory of both my mother, Agnes, whose dedication as a writer continues to inspire me, and my father, Joseph, who graduated as an officer in May 1943 from the Naval Officer Training School at the University of Notre Dame, for valiant service at Normandy and Okinawa.

In addition, I extend my gratitude to the parishioners of Little Flower Parish in Bethesda, Maryland, where I am presently pastor, and to the members of the John Carroll Society for whom I have served as chaplain.

Special gratitude to my family, to my editor Robert M. Hamma, to Gerald O'Collins, S.J., Monsignor Kevin Hart, Adoreen McCormick, and Kevin J. McIntyre, who provided valuable assistance with the text.

CONTENTS

FOREWORD

As the pastor of a large and thriving parish, Monsignor Peter J. Vaghi has many opportunities to teach, lead and sanctify the faithful entrusted to his care. *The Faith We Profess: A Catholic Guide to the Apostles' Creed* is a testimony to Monsignor Vaghi's profound commitment to be a teacher of the faith for his people. Pastors teach in various ways, but Monsignor Vaghi has set an example of providing careful instruction in an engaging style that brings the reader through the articles of the creed in a manner that is inviting in its presentation and informative in its content.

What is evident in this book, which is a collection of reflections Monsignor Vaghi has offered his parishioners, are his many years of experience in explaining the faith to those whom he shepherds. One has the sense in reading this book that Monsignor Vaghi is responding to questions and inquiries, observations and the experiences of his parishioners.

What characterizes this work is its ability to present the doctrine found in the *Catechism of the Catholic Church* as well as in the *United States Catholic Catechism for Adults* in clear and popular language. It thus becomes a timely contribution to our Church's mission of a new evangelization. In concise, easy-to-understand language, Monsignor Vaghi explains how the content of the catechisms on the universal and national level touch our lives. He uses the words of Sacred Scripture, examples from everyday life and his own extensive pastoral experience to delve more deeply into each of the articles of the Creed in a way that makes them come alive.

One can think of any number of ways in which this book will be helpful, but two come immediately to mind. Adult faith formation is increasingly a significant part of the ministry of the Church especially at the parish level. This book is a rich resource for parish adult faith formation programs and, in a special way, for the Rite of Christian Initiation for Adults. In this area where there is a recognized need to provide a systematic presentation of the faith, Monsignor Vaghi's book presents an ideal companion for those making the faith journey that will bring them to the Easter sacraments of initiation.

Another area where *The Faith We Profess* can be of immeasurable assistance is with the ever increasing number of Catholics interested in knowing more about their faith so that they can be a voice of the faith in our world today, prepared to bear witness among their peers, friends, and associates to the truth and meaning of the Church's teaching. Increasingly, in response to the pressures of an ever more secular culture, many Catholic women and men are looking for clear, well written, concise, and engaging material that can better form them to be witnesses to the faith in their many and varied circumstances. This book is an answer to that need. Monsignor Vaghi has done all of us engaged in the effort of proclaiming the faith a great service as we work to illuminate the richness of our Catholic faith and guide others to a deeper understanding and appreciation of the Church's message.

Most Reverend Donald W. Wuerl
Archbishop of Washington D.C.

An Introduction to
the Apostles' Creed

In a beautiful homily preached on September 12, 2006, in Regensburg, Germany, Pope Benedict XVI spoke of the Apostles' Creed as a *summa* or summary of everything we believe. He described how the Apostles' Creed is divided into twelve articles corresponding to the twelve apostles. He likewise observed that the Apostles' Creed is divided into three main sections referring to the Trinity and the baptismal formula: "I baptize you in the name of the Father, and of the Son, and of the Holy Spirit." The Apostles' Creed that we know today comes from an ancient creed used in Rome by candidates for Baptism when they professed their faith.

Hence, the Pope points out:

> The Creed is not a collection of propositions; it is not a theory. It is anchored in the event of Baptism—a genuine encounter between God and man. In the mystery of Baptism, God stoops to meet us; he comes close to us and in turn brings us closer to one another. Baptism means that Jesus Christ adopts us as his brothers and sisters, welcoming us as sons and daughters into God's family.

For Benedict, the creed is thus primarily an encounter with Christ and not just a way of expressing the contents of our faith.

> We have inherited two creeds from the early Church: the shorter Apostles' Creed that is derived from preparation for Baptism and took shape in the third century; and the longer Nicene-Constantinopolitan Creed (often called simply "the Nicene Creed") that is derived from two General

Councils of the Church held in Asia Minor: Nicea
I (325) and Constantinople I (381).

The Apostles' Creed was geared to the needs of those
preparing for Baptism. The Nicene Creed confronted errors
about Christ and the Holy Spirit and expressed the faith of all
Christians: that Christ is truly divine and truly human, and
that the Spirit is the divine guide of the Church. Used at the
Eucharist in all the churches of Eastern and Western Christianity, the Nicene Creed expresses the way "from east to west
a perfect offering" is made "to the glory" of God's name (Eucharistic Prayer III).

Perhaps you have not reflected or meditated on our faith—
the "contents" of the faith—in recent years. It is so easy to take
faith for granted, to forget that it is more than an academic or
theoretical exercise. Each Sunday, after the homily, we recite
the Nicene Creed—sometimes without really thinking about
it. How often do we recall that our profession of faith is a
fundamental life decision that we renew each Sunday and
one that has consequences for how we live our lives and the
choices we make?

Or perhaps you are new to the Catholic faith, preparing
for Baptism or for full communion with the Church. In this
case, the faith may be fresh and challenging to you. As you
are guided through the various stages of the Rite of Christian
Initiation of Adults (RCIA) you will become more familiar
with the Apostles' Creed. Before being baptized on Holy Saturday at the Easter Vigil, you will be questioned as to whether
you are willing to profess the various articles of the creed. In
Baptism, you who are catechumens will pledge yourself to
Christ and accept the basic Christian belief in him, as well as
in God the Father and the Holy Spirit. Those of you who are
welcomed into full communion with the Church, and all of
us who are already Catholics—whether baptized as children
or adults—will renew our baptismal vows by responding, "I
believe," to questions drawn from the Apostles' Creed.

Whether the faith is familiar or new to you, the words spoken by our Holy Father Benedict XVI at a conference in northern Italy in 2007 are most valuable:

> Our faith is well founded; but it is necessary that this faith become part of our lives. A great effort must therefore be made in order for all Christians to transform themselves into "witnesses," ready and able to shoulder the commitment of testifying—always and to everyone—to the hope that animates them.

Living our faith in this way "is possible only by grace and the interior helps of the Holy Spirit" (CCC 154).

Throughout this book, we will study each of the twelve articles of the Apostles' Creed. We will also see how the Apostles' Creed is trinitarian in format with three sections focusing in turn on the Father, the Son and the Holy Spirit.

• • •

This book draws fundamentally from three sources: the first part of the *Catechism of the Catholic Church* (CCC), published in 1997 and often referred to in the book as "the Catechism"; the first part of the *United States Catholic Catechism for Adults* (USCCA) promulgated by the American bishops in 2006; and the teachings of Pope John Paul II (1978–2005) and Pope Benedict XVI (elected in 2005). Each source can help us grow in faith and holiness. A list of abbreviations and references for quoted matter can be found in the back of the book.

The Apostles' Creed

I believe in God,
   the Father almighty,
creator of heaven and earth.

I believe in Jesus Christ, his only
   Son, our Lord.

He was conceived by the
   power of the Holy Spirit
   and born of the Virgin Mary.

He suffered under Pontius Pilate,
   was crucified, died, and was buried.
   He descended into hell.

On the third day he rose again.

He ascended into heaven
   and is seated at the right
   hand of the Father.
   He will come again to judge the
   living and the dead.

The Nicene Creed

We believe in one God,
   the Father, the Almighty,
   maker of heaven and earth,
   of all that is, seen and unseen.

We believe in one Lord, Jesus
      Christ,
   the only Son of God,
   eternally begotten of the Father,
   God from God, Light from Light,
   true God from true God,
   begotten, not made, one in Being
      with the Father.
   Through him all things were made.
   For us men and for our
      salvation
      he came down from heaven:
by the power of the Holy Spirit
   he was born of the Virgin Mary,
   and became man.

For our sake he was crucified
      under Pontius Pilate;
   he suffered, died, and was buried.

On the third day he rose again
      in fulfillment of the Scriptures;

he ascended into heaven
      and is seated at the right
      hand of the Father.
He will come again in glory to
      judge the living and the dead,
   and his kingdom will have no end

The Apostles' Creed

I believe in the Holy Spirit,
    the holy catholic Church,
    the communion of saints,
    the forgiveness of sins,
    the resurrection of the body,
    and the life everlasting. Amen.

The Nicene Creed

We believe in the Holy Spirit,
    the Lord, the giver of Life,
    who proceeds from the
      Father and the Son.
With the Father and the Son
    he is worshiped and
    glorified.
He has spoken through the
    Prophets.
We believe in one holy
    catholic and apostolic Church.
We acknowledge one
    baptism for the forgiveness
    of sins.
We look for the resurrection of
    the dead,
and the life of the world to
    come. Amen.

Prologue:
Pursued by the Hound of Heaven

Each of us thirsts for God, whether we are preparing for Baptism or have been baptized years ago. We all have both the capacity and the desire for God. At every stage in life's pilgrimage, God comes to meet us. And at every stage we are called to respond with the obedience of faith.

Our Capacity for God

A number of years ago, I made a pilgrimage in the footsteps of Saint Paul. On a very hot August day, Cardinal Pio Laghi and I climbed a steep and rocky hill in Athens to get a glimpse of the Areopagus or Mars Hill, where in AD 51 Saint Paul gave his famous "Men of Athens" speech. It was a speech delivered to lawyers, judges, and philosophers of his day (none of them schooled in the teaching or person of Jesus). It is referred to in paragraph 28 of the Catechism and enshrined forever in Acts 17:22–31.

It was there on Mars Hill that Saint Paul referred to this gathering of the Greek intelligentsia, at this cultural center of Athens, as "religious people." Paul addressed them: "You Athenians, I see that in every respect you are very religious. For as I walked around looking carefully at your shrines, I even discovered an altar inscribed 'To an Unknown God.'" What does this mean? It does not mean that they were religious in belief or practice as we profess to be. They were not. But they were religious in the deepest sense of that word, and Paul, even using language from one of their own pagan poets, tried to explain to them the living God. In his encyclical *Faith and Reason*, John Paul II referred to that speech and said: "The Apostle accentuates a truth which the Church has always treasured: in the far reaches of the human heart there is a seed of desire and nostalgia for God" (FR 24). The psalmist writes: "As the deer longs for streams of water, / so my soul longs for you, O God" (Ps 42:2).

The majority of Athenians were not open to what Paul had to say or to his efforts to bring them to accept the living God. And so he left. This experience is one known so often to each of us—at work, at social gatherings, even in our homes—wherever the Areopagus of our day may be. The God who means so much to us can leave others unmoved and untouched.

In an interview with the media before his 2006 trip to his German homeland, Pope Benedict XVI had this to say:

> It's become more difficult to believe because the world in which we find ourselves is completely made up of ourselves, and God . . . doesn't appear directly anymore. We don't drink from the source anymore, but from the vessel which is offered to us already full, and so on. Humanity has rebuilt the world by itself, and finding God inside this world has become more difficult.

This should not be cause for discouragement. As in the time of ancient Athens, whether or not Jesus Christ is explicitly acknowledged as Lord and Savior, a desire and a quest for God are written in every human heart without exception. That is so precisely because we are created by God and for God. In that same interview, Pope Benedict also stated more positively:

> The quest for "something bigger" wells up again from the depths of western people. We see how in young people there is a search for something "more"; we see how the religious phenomenon is returning, even if that search is rather indefinite. But with all this the Church is present once more,

and faith is offered as the answer. This visit . . . is
an opportunity to help people see that believing
is beautiful, that the joy of a huge universal community possesses a transcendent strength, that behind this belief lies something important, and that
together with the new movements there are also
new outlets in the search for the faith that lead us
from one to the other. These are positive develop-
ments for society as a whole.

The *United States Catholic Catechism for Adults* addresses
the fact that a large number of people are coming to the faith
yearly through the RCIA. "It is encouraging that many are
finding the move to secularism to be an unsatisfactory approach and continue to search for a deeper meaning in life"
(*USCCA* 6).

In his day, speaking of the Lord in his own language, Saint
Augustine wrote similarly: "Our hearts are restless until they
rest in you." God never ceases drawing us to himself, even
when he is not explicitly known to us. God has written the
desire to know him upon our very hearts.

Pope John Paul II expressed this quite eloquently: "God
has placed in the human heart a desire to know the truth—
in a word, to know himself—so that, by knowing and loving
God, men and women may also come to the fullness of truth
about themselves." In his encyclical *The Splendor of Truth*, he
similarly stated: "In the depths of His heart there always remains a yearning for absolute truth and a thirst to attain full
knowledge of it. This is eloquently proved by man's tireless
search for knowledge in all fields" (*VS* 1). In this sense we are
religious by nature, for we are created to transcend ourselves.
"Human beings would not even begin to search for something of which they knew nothing or for something which
they thought was wholly beyond them. Only the sense that
they can arrive at an answer leads them to take the first step"
(*FR* 29).

This step, this search, is one thing. But how do we come to know and discover and even love God? There are two ways: by looking at creation—the physical world and the human person—and by listening to God's revelation. The first way is an act of reason; the second is an act of religion. The first way is open to all humanity; the second only to those who hear the good news of Christ and become believers. What we discover by the first way is called the law of nature or natural law; what we discover by the second way is the law of Christ or the law of the gospel.

The Church teaches that God can be known with certainty from the created world by the natural light of human reason. Without this innate capacity, we would not be in a position to welcome God's revelation. Each of us has this capacity precisely because we are created in the "image of God." This doctrine, called the "natural means" of coming to know God, is of great importance. It is the presupposition for the Church's dialogue with all men and women regardless of their religious background. It justifies the confidence that it is possible to speak to all men and women about God. But note well—our human words always fall short in their ability to speak about the mystery of God. To be able to enter into real intimacy with God, moreover, our creator willed both to reveal himself and to give us the grace that empowers us to accept this revelation in faith.

God Comes to Meet Us

What then is revelation? It is the personal self-communication in history of a living God to us, a communication that always depends on his initiative. Reason is simply not enough, for through reason we cannot know God's inner life nor his loving plan for us personally. Revelation is another order of knowledge that we cannot arrive at on our own. It operates on the level of God's freely given grace.

Revelation comes through the words and actions of a living God—our God. "In Revelation, the tremendous gulf between God and the human race is bridged" (*USCCA* 13). In the words of Vatican Council II, the divine plan of salvation is realized simultaneously "by deeds and words which are intrinsically bound up with each other" and shed light on each other (*DV* 2). There are various stages of revelation, recorded in Sacred Scripture, that have taken centuries to unfold. "God's Revelation disturbed and changed the patriarchs, prophets, Apostles and others"—from Moses to Isaiah to Peter himself (*USCCA* 14). God communicates, reveals, unpacks, unveils himself gradually and continually, culminating in the person and mission of his Son Jesus Christ, and he continues to do so through the power of the Holy Spirit in our day. But note well that "no new public revelation is to be expected before the glorious manifestation of our Lord, Jesus Christ (cf. 1 Tim 6:14 and Tit 2:13)" (*DV* 4). The divine revelation ceaselessly addresses the Church at large and individuals in particular, but does not add anything to the essential truth revealed by Jesus Christ and the coming of the Holy Spirit.

John Paul II wrote: "In the Incarnation of the Son of God we see forged the enduring and definitive synthesis which the human mind of itself could not even have imagined: the Eternal enters time, the Whole lies hidden in the part, God takes on a human face" (*FR* 12). He is the definitive revelation of God. It is "only in the mystery of the incarnate Word" that "the mystery of man" is disclosed (*GS* 22). Seen in any other terms, the mystery of personal existence remains an insoluble riddle. "Where might the human being seek the answer to dramatic questions such as pain, the suffering of the innocent and death, if not in the light streaming from the mystery of Christ's Passion, Death and Resurrection?" (*FR* 12). God continues to reveal himself to us, to invite us to enter into his life, the life of the Father, Son, and Holy Spirit, to make himself present in our lives often when we least expect him. "God comes to us in the things we know best and can verify most easily, the things of our everyday life, apart from which we cannot understand ourselves" (FR 12).

Our God is a God of surprises, persistent and often unexpected. Remember the persistence, the sound and the movement that the English poet Francis Thompson calls "the Hound of Heaven." And oh how we react in different ways at different times of our lives! Francis Thompson captured God and our reaction so well:

I fled Him, down the nights and down the days;
   I fled Him, down the arches of the years;
I fled Him, down the labyrinthine ways
   Of my own mind; and in the midst of tears
I hid from Him, and under running laughter.
     Up vistaed hopes I sped;
     And shot, precipitated,
Adown Titanic glooms of chasmèd fears,
   From those strong Feet that followed, followed after.
     But with unhurrying chase,
     And unperturbèd pace,
Deliberate speed, majestic instancy,
    They beat—and a Voice beat
     More instant than the Feet—
"All things betray thee, who betrayest Me."

In the words of the Book of Revelation, "Behold, I stand at the door and knock. If anyone hears my voice and opens the door, [then] I will enter his house and dine with him, and he with me" (Rev 3:20). And how can we forget the parable about the shepherd searching for the lost sheep? "And when he does find it, he sets it on his shoulders with great joy" (Lk 15:5).

Our God continues to speak to us. Do we listen? Do we hear him amidst the din of our daily existence and all the challenges and noise? Do we make time for him? He so wants to speak and desires that we listen each day.

There is the living and life-giving Word of God, his Word that continues to invite us to listen, his Word revealed in Sacred Scripture and the living Tradition of the Church. Listen closely to his living Word, a Word that informs, changes, and criticizes us, strengthens and gives life and forms us more and more into Christ himself.

The changes in the liturgy implemented by the Second Vatican Council have led to a deeper appreciation of Sacred Scripture in the life of the Church. Frequent prayerful reading and study of the Bible is essential to growth in the Lord. It is an integral part of our lives as Catholics. Saint Jerome has reminded us that "ignorance of the Scriptures is ignorance of Christ" (*DV* 25). Sacred Scripture, both the Old and New Testament, is the speech of God as it is put down in writing under the breath of the Holy Spirit—forty-six books of the Old Testament and twenty-seven books of the New Testament. These books, which form the canon or authoritative books of the Bible, were identified in the early centuries of the Church as having been divinely inspired.

Unlike the fundamentalists, however, ours is not a faith that relies solely on Scripture for revelation. Ours is a faith that includes Tradition, a living transmission distinct from Scripture but never separated from Scripture. Through Tradition, the Church, in her doctrine, life, and worship, perpetuates and transmits to every generation all that she herself is and all that she believes through the reception of the sacraments, the teaching of the Holy Father and our bishops, our common prayer, and in other ways. As we study prayerfully at this very moment, we are experiencing the living Tradition of the Church, the living voice of the Lord himself. God is speaking to us in a very special way in the quiet of our prayer where he breaks out into our lives.

God's Word is recorded and interpreted in the inspired Scripture, and then transmitted, interpreted, and applied by the living Tradition of the Church. Thus Tradition has its source in the revelation of the Word of God. We can never forget as well that the task of giving an authentic interpretation to the Word of God has been entrusted to the living, teaching office of the Church, which is called the Magisterium—the Pope and the bishops in communion with him. The Magisterium is not superior to the Word of God but its servant, the servant of truth.

Reflect

1. Saint Augustine, a fourth-century convert, bishop, and Father of the Church, wrote at the beginning of his classic work *The Confessions*: "You have made us for yourself, O Lord, and our hearts are restless until they rest in you."

   Do you experience restlessness? What do you do with this feeling?

2. There are two ways that we can come to know and love God. The first is by looking at creation—the physical world and the human person.

   In what ways does the natural world reveal God to you? How does it obscure God?

   What human quality is for you the most tangible sign of God? And what human quality most challenges your faith in God?

3. The second way we come to know God is by revelation. Revelation is the personal self-communication in history of a living God to us, a communication that always depends on God's

initiative.

How does God reveal himself to you in Scripture?

How do you experience God in the Church?

4. What else in this chapter was important to you?

Pray

Late have I loved you,
O Beauty ever ancient, ever new,
late have I loved you!
You were within me, but I was outside,
and it was there that I searched for you.
In my unloveliness
I plunged into the lovely things which you created.
You were with me, but I was not with you.
Created things kept me from you;
yet if they had not been in you
they would not have been at all.
You called, you shouted,
and you broke through my deafness.
You flashed, you shone,
and you dispelled my blindness.
You breathed your fragrance on me;
I drew in breath and now I pant for you.
I have tasted you,
now I hunger and thirst for more.
You touched me,
and I burned for your peace.

—From *The Confessions* of Saint Augustine

ONE

I Believe in God, the Father Almighty, Creator of Heaven and Earth

I Believe

*F*aith is a response word. It is our human response to God, who continues to reveal and communicate his love to us. It is our free response to a loving God. In every moment of each day, God continually reveals himself through the living scripture and the ongoing life of the Church that we call Tradition—the prayer life, the sacramental life, and the teaching life of the Church as given us by our Pope and the bishops.

Faith has two aspects. It is at once a response to a person, to Jesus, and it is a response to the message that Jesus teaches in and through the Church. Not unlike two sides of the same coin, it is at once what I believe, the content of faith, and at the same time it is the act of personal surrender to the God encountered now in and through Jesus Christ, the person to whom I submit my life. Such surrender engages the whole person.

In his visit to Poland in May 2006, Pope Benedict XVI spoke frequently about faith, encouraging the Polish people to stand firm in the faith. In his homily of May 28, 2006, in Kraków, he said: "To believe means first to accept as true

what our mind cannot fully comprehend. We have to accept
what God reveals to us about himself, about ourselves, about
everything around us, including the things that are invisible,
inexpressible, and beyond our imagination." The Pope spoke
of the second aspect of the faith in these words: "It is trust in
a person, no ordinary person, but Jesus Christ himself. What
we believe is important, but even more important is the One
in whom we believe. . . . Believing means surrendering ourselves to God and entrusting our destiny to him . . . and making this relationship the basis of our whole life." Two days
prior in Warsaw he had said, "Faith does not just mean accepting a certain number of abstract truths about the mysteries of God, of man, of life and death, of future realities. Faith
consists in an intimate relationship with Christ, a relationship
based on love of him who loved us first, even to the total offering of himself."

This response of faith calls us to bear witness by word and
deed. The response of faith is not lifeless or merely academic.
Faith is very practical. It is the criterion that actually deter-
mines and defines our lifestyles. It often demands sacrifice
and invites ridicule. You and I know this from our experience
of trying to live our daily lives at home and in the workplace.
Nor does faith mean anything without love.

Saint Ignatius of Antioch, who died in Rome around AD
107, was one of many in the history of the Church who let
himself be torn to pieces by the jaws of lions in the Roman
arena rather than reject his faith. Cardinal John Henry Newman (1801–90) once wrote: "No one is a martyr for a conclusion, no one is a martyr for an opinion; it is faith that makes
us martyrs." It is faith in a living person, in Jesus Christ. After
all, we do not give our lives to a question mark.

Abraham and Moses have given us outstanding examples
of faith. Our Blessed Lady even more so embodies the obedience of faith. Mary puts flesh on what could be simply an
abstract concept. That is why the Church venerates her in a

very special way. In Mary, we see the purest realization of faith. She truly heard and listened to God's Word brought by an angel, and she surrendered to that Word. She had no idea where it would lead her, but she trusted in God's Word. At the Annunciation, she listened and was moved to consent. At its heart, this is faith. Mary remained faithful so that she said: "May it be done to me according to your word" (Lk 1:38).

Faith is both a grace of God, a gift of God's love, an impulse of the Holy Spirit, *and at the same time* a free human act. It is a task. If it were not a grace, it could not reach God himself. If it were not a human act, a task, it would not be a real answer. It involves an assent of both the intellect and the will to God's self-revelation, communicated to us in words and deeds.

Faith is necessary for our salvation, and even though there is salvation outside the Catholic Church, it is through Christ's Catholic Church alone that the fullness of the means of salvation can be obtained. The Lord himself affirms: "Whoever believes and is baptized will be saved; whoever does not believe will be condemned" (Mk 16:16). Faith is a foretaste of the beatific vision that is the goal of our journey on earth. "The ultimate goal of a life of faith is eternal union with God in heaven" (*USCCA* 41).

Faith requires perseverance. It grows in stages. Often we must crawl before we can walk. Sometimes we fall and walk again. It seems that so often faith must withstand various tests and even scandals. Each one of us knows that. And we are not in it alone. The Catechism reminds us: "To live, grow and persevere in the faith until the end we must nourish it with the word of God; we must beg the Lord to increase our faith (cf. Mk 9:24; Lk 17:5; 22:32); it must be 'working through charity,' abounding in hope, and rooted in the faith of the Church (Gal 5:6; Rom 15:13; cf. Jas 2:14–26)" (*CCC* 162).

The Church's faith, the faith that has perdured for centuries, precedes, engenders, supports, and nourishes our faith.

Faith is not just a private act. "In the assembly of believers at Mass, we profess our faith together and join our hearts as we experience ourselves as the Body of Christ" (*USCCA* 37).

Our faith is reasonable. We have "a reason for [our] hope" (1 Pt 3:15). It is not unreasonable, for instance, to believe in the existence of God and to believe that we all come from God and are going to God. The created world and our experiences in life offer us many hints of God. We can reasonably say: "In him we live and move and have our being" (Acts 17:28). Yet faith leads us beyond what is merely reasonable. There are good reasons for accepting God our Creator and Jesus Christ, whom he has sent.

Finally, the response of faith does not complete the journey that reason began with its initial questions: Who am I? Where have I come from? Where I am going? Why is there suffering or evil? Is there life after death? It helps us, however, to realize that our response of faith is just the beginning of a journey that will continue throughout our lives.

John Paul II eloquently stated:

> Men and women are on a journey of discovery which is humanly unstoppable—a search for the truth and a search for a person to whom they might entrust themselves. Christian faith comes to meet them, offering the concrete possibility of reaching the goal which they seek. Moving beyond the stage of simple believing, Christian faith immerses human beings in the order of grace, which . . . , in turn offers them a true and coherent knowledge of the Triune God. In Jesus Christ, who is the Truth, faith recognizes the ultimate appeal to humanity, an appeal made in order that what we experience as desire and nostalgia may come to fulfillment. (*FR* 33)

In summary, our faith is fundamentally a response word. Faith is at once a response to a person, to the person Jesus, and it is a response to the message that Jesus teaches in and through his Church. It is the "what" of our belief and, at the same time, it is the personal surrender to our God, two sides of the same coin. To believe is at once a human act and an act continually inspired by the Holy Spirit. Both are required for the faith response.

In God

In the Apostles' Creed we say, "I believe in God"; while in the Nicene Creed we say, "We believe in one God." Each Sunday at Mass we make this significant affirmation of our faith in one God as a community of believers. How often do we ponder its implications for our lives, this belief in *one* God? This first affirmation of the Apostles' Creed is also the most fundamental. All other articles depend on this first one and help us to know God better as he progressively reveals himself to us in creation and as Trinity: Father, Son, and Holy Spirit. "Revelation tells us that he is living and personal, profoundly close to us in creating and sustaining us" (*USCCA* 51). "The mystery of the Most Holy Trinity is the central mystery of the Christian faith and of Christian life" (*CCC* 261). The inner life of God consists of the relationship of infinite love among the Father, the Son, and the Holy Spirit. This tri-personal God has been revealed as the God who is with us and for us.

Even though we profess a belief in God, and most people do, there is still a fundamental "holy" mystery about him, about the sense of the sacred—particularly in our increasingly secular society. Our God is at once close at hand, present to us in the peace of our prayer and in sacramental encounters, and at the same time seemingly distant. Through the prophet Isaiah, God continues to invite us to "turn to [him] and be safe"

(Is 45:22). We are called to turn away from the many "gods" of our culture, the gods of wealth, power, success, and sex, and to worship the one true God.

Where is it that you meet God in your life? Where do you become reassured of his constant and mysterious presence and love for you? He revealed himself to the Chosen People slowly and progressively throughout their history. Do you approach him like Moses at the burning bush, on the threshold of the Exodus and the Sinai covenant, and ask him his name? (Ex 3:1–15). Knowing the name of a person, in the biblical understanding of *name*, communicates the very identity and meaning of a person's life. In effect, one's name encompasses the person. God is, after all, not an anonymous force or a vague destiny. He is a living God. He has a history of speaking to his people, to the people he has chosen, a history that has been interpreted and recorded through the inspired Bible. God is a person; he has a name and an identity.

God responded to Moses, "I am who am" (Ex 3:14). Only God can define himself by saying, "I am." In revealing this mysterious name, which in Hebrew is "Yahweh," he reveals himself uniquely as the God who is always there, faithfully present to his people from the very beginning and throughout the future, the one true, compassionate, and living God. At the same time, God remains a holy mystery. At the burning bush, Moses took off his sandals out of respect and veiled his face in the presence of God's holiness. How do we show respect in the presence of our God? Do we genuflect before the tabernacle? Are we silent in his presence? We are not his equals. He is all-holy and faithful despite our imperfections and sin, as he was faithful to Israel despite their repeated sinfulness and the lack of faithfulness—our God is "rich in mercy."

Above all else, the answer to God's identity is love. Love is another name for God. Israel came to understand this reality throughout her long history. Sheer gratuitous love—that is God. God's love is everlasting. It is the love that ultimately sent his Son to die for us that we might share his eternal life. His very being is steadfast love.

The Father

Jesus called God "Father." He revealed God as Father "in a new sense" (*USCCA* 52), indeed "an unheard-of sense" (*CCC* 240). "Father" is a translation of *Abba,* a word in Aramaic, the mother tongue of Jesus, that can also be translated as "Daddy dear." What a contrast to Moses' experience, where the emphasis was on the otherness of God: "'Come no nearer! Remove the sandals from your feet, for the place where you stand is holy ground.' . . . Moses hid his face, for he was afraid to look at God" (Ex 3:5–6).

The Catechism teaches that despite the paternal tenderness of our God, this certainly can also be expressed by the image of motherhood, despite the truth that God transcends the human distinction between the sexes, and despite the fact that God is neither man nor woman. Jesus taught us that God is Father in a unique way. No one is father as God is Father. He is eternally Father by his relationship to his only Son, who, reciprocally, is Son only in relation to his Father. "No one knows the Son except the Father, and no one knows the Father except the Son and anyone to whom the Son wishes to reveal him" (Mt 11:27).

In this section on God as Father, the Catechism immediately places its emphasis on God as triune: God who is Father, but God who is also Son and Holy Spirit. The Catechism speaks of the Holy Trinity, this most fundamental and challenging truth of our faith, in a very profound way. It is central to the Catechism and central to our faith—the triune existence of God.

Every aspect of our sacramental life and our prayer is influenced by the trinitarian dimension of our faith. It begins at

Baptism. You remember, if not from your own Baptism, certainly from baptisms that you have attended, how the priest or deacon asks a series of questions about the Trinity: "Do you believe in God, the Father almighty, Creator of heaven and earth?" Then he asks questions about Jesus and about the Holy Spirit. After each question, the one to be baptized or the parents and godparents respond: "I do." These questions mirror the same trinitarian formula that is used when Baptism is conferred: "I baptize you in the name of the Father, and of the Son, and of the Holy Spirit." At that moment, we are called to share in the very life of the Godhead forever—becoming children of God the Father, members of the body of Christ, and temples of the Holy Spirit. Each of us is made in the image and likeness of God, redeemed by the blood of Christ, and made holy by the presence of the Holy Spirit. The life of the Trinity is alive in each of us.

> The mystery of the Most Holy Trinity is the central mystery of Christian faith and life. It is the mystery of God in himself. It is therefore the source of all the other mysteries of faith, the light that enlightens them. It is the most fundamental and essential teaching in the "hierarchy of the truths of faith." (CCC 234, quoting General Catechetical Directory 43)

The Catechism further explains this mystery:

> The Trinity is One. We do not confess three Gods, but one God in three persons, the "consubstantial Trinity. [Footnote: Council of Constantinople II (553): DS 421.]" The divine persons do not share the one divinity among themselves but each of them is God whole and entire: "The Father is that which the Son is, the Son is that which the Father is, the Father and the Son that which the Holy

Spirit is i.e. by nature one God [Footnote: Council
of Toledo XI (675): *DS* 530:26]." (*CCC* 253)

This sublime mystery is inaccessible to reason alone. Traces of the mystery of the Holy Trinity are hidden in the work of creation and revealed in the Old Testament. But it was the sending of Jesus and the Holy Spirit that revealed fully the triune nature of God. We would not have understood God as Father if it had not been for Jesus or God the Holy Spirit, if Jesus had not spoken of the Advocate who would be sent. "But I tell you the truth, it is better for you that I go. For if I do not go, the Advocate will not come to you. But if I go, I will send him to you" (Jn 16:7).

Saint Augustine described the Holy Spirit as the Love between the Father and the Son. In the power of the Holy Spirit, you and I are actually brought into the very intimate life of God, and into that relationship between the Father and the Son. A sublime community constitutes the life of the Trinity and models for us true communal love. If God is a community of persons, then we should also seek to imitate this divine community. That is how God is revealed to others in and through each of us and our love for each other—precisely in relationship. Cardinal Walter Kasper writes: "Only because God is love within himself can he be love for us. . . . Love is that which reconciles unity and multiplicity; it is the uniting unity in the threeness."

In fact, the whole of the Christian life is an invitation to communion with the unity of the Blessed Trinity, here on earth in the obscurity of faith and after death in eternal light: "Whoever loves me will keep my word," says the Lord, "and my Father will love him, and we will come to him and make our dwelling with him" (Jn 14:23).

Almighty

"Of all the divine attributes, only God's omnipotence is named in the Creed" (*CCC* 268). His might is universal, loving, and mysterious. Mary's Magnificat, proclaimed each day in the Liturgy of the Hours, beautifully confirms this quality of God when she proclaims:

> The Almighty has done great things for me. . . .
> He has shown the strength of his arm,
> he has scattered the proud in their conceit.
> He has cast down the mighty from their thrones,
> and has lifted up the lowly.
> He has filled the hungry with good things,
> and the rich he has sent away empty. (Lk 1:49–53)

And yet in the face of the almighty power of God, the Catechism speaks of the mystery of the apparent powerlessness of God. Our faith in God is put to the test by the experience of evil and suffering. God can sometimes seem to be absent and incapable of stopping evil and suffering. We often ask how such bad things can happen to good people—a young son who is killed in a car accident, or a husband who loses his wife to illness at an early age. Where is God the almighty in all of this?

In their book *Believing: Understanding the Creed*, Gerald O'Collins, S.J., and Mary Venturini offer an answer to this perplexing challenge about the omnipotence of our God:

> One of the most simple answers must be that God is not a celluloid Superman who holds up crumbling dams, pastes back the earthquake cracks, forces missiles off their path, stops helicopters crashing to the ground and kills the terrible tyrant just in time to save mankind from disaster. Superman is the modern projection of human wishes and needs, of our longing for supernatural happenings. God is

not. Superman would certainly have escaped from the cross, saved the two thieves along with him, rustled up the trembling apostles to defeat the Roman legions and converted the world to instant goodness. God did not and left us limited human beings wondering why.

Only faith can embrace the mysterious ways of God's almighty power, a faith that unceasingly holds that nothing is impossible with God, even a God who embraces suffering himself, raises suffering to the level of our redemption and remains almighty nonetheless. God seems always to be on the side of suffering. The greatest paradox is that his omnipotence is manifested precisely in the fact that he freely accepted suffering out of love, love for you and me. "He shows almighty power by converting us from our sins and by restoring us to grace" (USCCA 62).

Suffering is both a challenge and an opportunity. Suffering makes sense and has power only when we see in it the mystery of the Cross and resurrection of Jesus Christ. Apart from Christ, suffering remains a problem without a solution. But when we experience in our suffering the power of the Lord—precisely in our weakness, in our own struggles, or in the struggles and suffering of others—we begin to understand this fundamental mystery of our faith. That takes time and is a gradual process.

Creator

In sovereign freedom and out of nothing, God has brought about and constantly maintains in existence all that is. This is the Christian understanding of creation. "The whole creation proclaims the greatness of your glory," we proclaim in the Liturgy of the Hours.

In God, "we live and move and have our being" (Acts 17:28). The Catechism teaches that "God alone created the universe freely, directly, and without any help" (CCC 317). God created everything out of nothing: "Look at the heavens and the earth and see all that is in them; then you will know that God did not make them out of existing things; and in the same way the human race came into existence" (2 Mc 7:28).

"In the beginning, . . . God created the heavens and the earth" (Gn 1:1). This is the very first sentence of the Bible. The question of creation has concerned humanity from the very beginning: Where do we all come from? What is our purpose? Although there are many theories, scientific and mythological, the Christian sees in creation the first and universal witness to God's almighty love and his wisdom. Creation conveys the first proclamation of God's plan of loving goodness, which finds its goal in the new creation in Christ. All reality, all life, and above all, all intelligent life come from God.

Scientific observation and reason can explore and reach well-founded conclusions about the evolution of various forms of life. But there is also another aspect to creation: elements of mystery that must be explored. O'Collins and Venturini write:

> The essence of creation is not something that can be restrained within the bounds of scientific theory, however much we may long for an easy, provable formula. Each act of creation, whether a new human being, work of art or scientific theory, is unique. A part is explainable in scientific, biological or technical terms but a part is not. A great painting is no more reducible to the artist and his materials than a new-born child is just the sum of its parents. The two are bound but they are separate; the hands of God and Adam on the ceiling of the Sistine Chapel reach for each other but they do not touch.

Although the first three chapters of the Book of Genesis occupy a special place among all the texts about creation, God also progressively revealed the mystery of creation throughout the history of the Hebrew people. From faith in God, whom they knew as active in their history and with whom they were bound through a special covenant, the Israelites also came to recognize God's hand in the making of the world. "Yours are the heavens, yours the earth; / you founded the world and everything in it" (Ps 89:12).

From the creative works of art to the sublime mystery of the birth of a child, it is clear that God calls on each of us to be co-creators with him. It is not a sign of his weakness but rather a token of God's almighty greatness and goodness. God created the world not to increase his glory but to show forth his glory and communicate his blessings to us. "Because creation comes forth from God's goodness, it shares in that goodness— 'And God saw that it was good . . . very good' (Gen 1:4, 10, 12, 18, 21, 31)" (CCC 299).

This raises the question of why, if God created a good and ordered world, evil exists. The Catechism admits that no quick answer will suffice. In fact, it states that only the Christian faith, as a whole, constitutes an answer to this perplexing riddle. "From the greatest moral evil ever committed—the rejection and murder of God's only Son, caused by the sins of all men—God, by his grace that 'abounded all the more,' (cf. Rom 5:20) brought the greatest of goods: the glorification of Christ and our redemption" (CCC 312).

The Catechism teaches that with infinite wisdom and goodness God freely willed to create a world "in a state of journeying" toward perfection—with the existence of the more perfect alongside the less perfect (CCC 302). Angels and human beings, as intelligent and free creatures, travel that journey by their free choice and preferential love. So important was free will, in fact a distinguishing characteristic of the human state, that God respects our freedom even to go astray.

In fact, "God permits such moral evil [e.g., the evil of sin] in part out of respect for the gift of freedom with which he endowed created beings" (*USCCA* 57).

God permits this because he respects our freedom and mysteriously knows even how to derive good from evil and life from death. We bury seeds in the earth and crops spring up. Through the pain of childbirth, women give rise to new human lives. Men and women perform extraordinary acts of fortitude that can cost much physical and mental suffering. Forgiveness can transform situations that seem terribly damaged and even destroyed by injustice and injury.

Above all: "Faith gives us the certainty that God would not permit an evil if he did not cause a good to come from that very evil, by ways that we shall fully know only in eternal life" (*CCC* 324).

Let us listen again to Benedict XVI's homily in Regensburg, Germany of September 12, 2006: "As Christians, we say: 'I believe in God the Father, the Creator of heaven and earth.' . . . With this faith we have no reason to hide, no fear of ending up in a dead end. We rejoice that we can know God! And we try to help others see the reasonableness of faith as Saint Peter in his First Letter explicitly urged the Christians of his time to do, and with them, ourselves as well" (cf. 1 Pt 3:15). Belief in God, after all, is our fundamental life decision.

Of Heaven and Earth

Where the Apostles' Creed speaks simply of the creation "of heaven and earth," the Nicene Creed develops this and states that God also created "all that is seen and unseen." In reflecting on this theme, the Catechism examines three important dimensions of faith: 1) the invisible world of angels and the visible world; 2) human beings as the summit of all creation; and 3) original sin and the fall.

The Invisible World of Angels

Did you know that 69 percent of those polled by *Time* magazine believed in the existence of angels, and that 46 percent of those polled believed they have a guardian angel? These interesting statistics were revealed in a popular cover story devoted to angels titled "Angels Among Us." I did a little poll myself. I asked a priest friend whether he believed in angels, and he quickly said yes. "I grew up in Saint Gabriel's Parish." Another friend of mine said yes. "I was born in Los Angeles—the City of Angels." Blessed John XXIII reportedly once said to a new bishop suffering from insomnia: "The very same thing happened to me in the first few weeks of my pontificate, but then one day my guardian angel appeared to me in a daydream and whispered: 'Giovanni, don't take yourself so seriously.' And ever since then I've been able to sleep."

Most of us who went to Catholic schools were taught to leave a little room at our desk for our guardian angels and were taught the prayer to our guardian angel. Remember it? "Angel of God, my guardian dear, to whom his love commits me here, ever this day (night) be at my side, to light and guard, to rule and guide. Amen."

Angels are quite popular today, especially during the Advent and Christmas seasons. One need only walk into any bookstore to see an entire section devoted to angels. There are "angels-only" boutiques, angel gift paper, angel newsletters, angel seminars, plays and movies and books about angels. Billy Graham's 1975 book, *Angels: God's Secret Agents*, was a national bestseller: 2.6 million copies sold. No pun intended, but angels are certainly in the air.

There is an extraordinary town and an abbey named after an angel off the coast of France, Mont-Saint-Michel.

> To the traveler, it first appears as a distant, gray, rough-cut diamond set in the silver sea. Mont-Saint-Michel, a town and an abbey improbably

perched on a rock off the coast of Normandy, presents itself in glimpses from bluffs along the coast road from Granville to Avranches. In medieval times, pilgrims flocked here to venerate the Archangel Michael. They did so at other European sites as well, but none of them casts a similar spell.

Why was it even built? Because "the Archangel loved heights," as Henry Adams contends in his opening line of his classic book *Mont-Saint-Michel and Chartres*. Legend has it that the Archangel Michael himself had a hand, or at least a finger, in it. According to legend, Saint Michael forcibly persuaded Bishop Aubert of Avranches in 708 to build an oratory dedicated to him on a rock known then as Mont Tombe. Reputedly, a hole penetrates the forehead of the bishop's skull where the Archangel had pressed his digit!

Why the general popularity of angels? As *Time* magazine noted: "For those who choke too easily on God and his rules, theologians observe, angels are the handy compromise, all fluff and meringue, kind, nonjudgmental. And they are available to everyone, like aspirin." Angels make only gentle demands on us and on our conduct.

The existence of angels is a truth of our faith. Created by God, they are "a realm of spiritual beings who do not share the limitations of a physical body and yet exist as the result of his all-powerful, loving act of creation"(*USCCA* 54). In fact, Jews, Christians, and Muslims, all three, affirm the existence of angels. There are also angels in scriptures of Buddhism, Hinduism, and Zoroastrianism. Cardinal Christoph Schönborn, O.P., in his book on the Catechism, writes: "The history of salvation is unthinkable apart from the angels."

The term *angel* means "messenger." Angels appear in more than half of the books of the Bible. They are purely spiritual creatures. They are servants and messengers of God who ceaselessly glorify him. Some of the angels turned against God and were driven to hell, their leader named Satan.

In Eucharistic Prayer IV, speaking to the Father, we pray: "Countless hosts of angels stand before you to do your will; they look upon your splendor and praise you, night and day." Angels are also with Christ. They are his angels. "From the Incarnation to the Ascension, the life of the Word incarnate is surrounded by the adoration and service of angels" (CCC 333). The angel Gabriel addresses Mary at the Annunciation: "Hail, favored one! The Lord is with you" (Lk 1:28). This scene, when an angel appeared to the Blessed Mother, has been portrayed repeatedly in religious artwork. Few scenes have been more celebrated by Christian artists. The words of the angel became part of our prayer—the Hail Mary. On Christmas night, the angels sang to the shepherds the well-known song of praise. "Their song of praise at the birth of Christ has not ceased resounding in the Church's praise: 'Glory to God in the highest' (Lk 2:14)" (CCC 333).

Not only do we repeat the words of the angels in our prayers and the liturgy, but "from its beginning until death, human life is surrounded by their watchful care and intercession" (CCC 336). Angels do exist. The Church venerates the angels who help her on her earthly pilgrimage and protect every human being.

The Visible World

God created not only the "invisible" but also the "visible" world in all its richness, diversity, and order, as is evident in the first two chapters of Genesis. "The sequence of creation reported in Chapter 1 of the Book of Genesis is not literal or scientific, but poetic and theological" (USCCA 55). The Catechism sets forth nine interpretative principles regarding

the visible world created by God with its variety and orders
of creatures:

1. "Nothing exists that does not owe its exis-
    tence to God the Creator" (CCC 338).

2. "Each creature possesses its own particu-
    lar goodness and perfection" and "reflects
    in its own way a ray of God's infinite wis-
    dom and goodness" (CCC 339).

3. "God wills the interdependence of crea-
    tures." No creature is self-sufficient.
    Hence nature mirrors the need for sharing
    and generosity" (CCC 340).

4. The beauty of the universe in all its diver-
    sity reflects the "infinite beauty of the Cre-
    ator" (CCC 341).

5. Although God loves all his creatures, Je-
    sus highlights an order of value within
    creation: "Of how much more value is a
    man than a sheep! (Lk 12:6–7; Mt 12:12)"
    (CCC 342).

6. Human beings are the summit of the Cre-
    ator's work.

7. "There is a *solidarity among all creatures*
    arising from the fact that all have the same
    Creator and all are ordered to his glory"
    (CCC 344).

8. The Creator "rested" on the Sabbath—a
    day of worship and adoration of God.
    Worship is thus inscribed in the very or-
    der of creation.

9. The eighth day, the day of Christ's resurrection, begins the new creation. The work
   of creation culminates in the greater work
   of redemption.

These principles thus help us to interpret the visible
world.

Humanity: Summit of All Creation

"God created man in his image; /in the divine image he
created him; /male and female he created them" (Gn 1:27).
Human beings therefore occupy a unique place in all of creation. Psalm 8:6 tells us that we are made a "little less than
a god." But what does it mean to be made in the image and
likeness of God? "God's image is a dynamic source of inner
spiritual energy drawing our minds and hearts toward truth
and love, and to God himself, the source of all truth and love"
(USCCA 67).

Ultimately, we are destined to reproduce the image of
God's Son made man, the "image of the invisible God" (Col
1:15). The Second Vatican Council teaches that "in reality it is
only in the mystery of the Word made flesh that the mystery
of man truly becomes clear" (GS 22). The foundation for all
Christian thinking about human life is based on this axiom
that each of us is created in the image and likeness of God and
that we are destined to share his life. "Of all visible creatures
only man is 'able to know and love his creator.' (GS 12 para.
3) . . . and he alone is called to share, by knowledge and love,
in God's own life. It was for this end that he was created, and
this is the fundamental reason for his dignity" (CCC 356).

This section of the Catechism on the dignity of the human
person refers ahead to paragraph 2258, which reads:

Human life is sacred because from its beginning it
involves the creative action of God and it remains

forever in a special relationship with the Creator, who is its sole end. God alone is the Lord of life from its beginning until its end: no one can under any circumstances claim for himself the right directly to destroy an innocent human being [Footnote: CDF, instruction, *Donum vitae*, intro. 5.].

Regrettably, however, we live in a world increasingly filled with contempt for the human person, a world filled with violence against the human person who is so often, too often, the object of such violence. One need only read the newspaper or watch daily television. The media is replete with examples of violence in the Middle East and other trouble spots around the world. The contempt for the human person today is evidenced by the millions of abortions, the advocacy for euthanasia and assisted suicide, the use of the death penalty to punish crime, and experimentation with stem cells that entails destroying fertilized embryos. The human person, the summit of all God's creation, is increasingly victimized. The dignity of the human person is indeed in jeopardy through false solutions or quick-fix methods. The Catechism teaches clearly: "Being in the image of God the human individual possesses the dignity of a person, who is not just something, but someone" (*CCC* 357). The Church will always be on the side of human life. Precisely because Jesus took on human life, he ennobled it and raised it to the level of a sharing in divine life.

Violence against the human person need not be deadly to be wrong. Anger and impatience are so often a challenge for each one of us in our daily lives and fast-moving society. Aggression (often displayed in our driving habits) and intolerance are likewise seeds of violence against the dignity of the human person. This kind of violence can be overcome, however, day by day, choice by choice, and person by person. "To be made in God's image also unites human beings as

God's stewards in the care of the earth and of all God's other creatures" (*USCCA* 67).

We are not alone in this endeavor to protect the dignity of the human person for, as the Catechism teaches: "Because of its common origin, *the human race forms a unity*" (*CCC* 360). Each of us is a brother and sister to one another. If only this teaching were appropriated in the Middle East and the other troubled spots of our world!

The Catechism teaches further that "the human person, created in the image of God, is a being at once corporeal and spiritual" (*CCC* 362). The human body has the dignity of being in the image of God, and it is a human body precisely because it is animated by a spiritual soul. The soul refers to the innermost aspect of human beings, that which is of greatest value. Although made of body and soul, they are a unity. No one may despise his bodily life. Rather everyone is obliged to regard his body as good and to hold it in honor since God has created it and will raise it up on the last day. The Church teaches that every spiritual soul is created immediately by God. "While our bodies come into being through physical processes, our souls are all created directly by God" (*USCCA* 68). They are immortal and will be reunited with the body at the final resurrection.

"Male and female he created them" (Gn 1:27). The Catechism underscores the equality of man and woman and their difference as willed by God. "Man and woman are both with one and the same dignity 'in the image of God' (cf. Gen 2:7, 22)" (*CCC* 369).

"God created man and woman together and willed each for the other" (*CCC* 371). He created them "to be a communion of persons, in which each can be 'helpmate' to the other, for they are equal as persons ('bone of my bones . . .') and complementary as masculine and feminine" (*CCC* 372). In marriage, God unites them in such a way that by forming "one flesh" they can transmit human life. Conception and childbirth are not curses. These make man and woman co-creators with God. In my marriage homilies, I love to quote from John Paul II's beautiful apostolic letter "On the Dignity and Vocation of Women," where he wrote about Christian marriage: "In the 'unity of two,' man and woman are called from the beginning not only to exist 'side by side' or 'together' but they are also called *to exist mutually 'one for the other'*"(*DM* 7).

Finally, the Church teaches that our first parents, Adam and Eve, were created in a state of original holiness and justice; they were created very good and established in friendship with God. As long as they remained intimate with God, they would neither suffer nor die. Work was not yet a burden. "This entire harmony of original justice, foreseen for man in God's plan, will be lost by the sin of our first parents" (*CCC* 379).

Original Sin and the Fall

Years ago, I heard a homily that has remained with me ever since. The homilist said that the two greatest events in the history of the world were the Fall of man and the redemption of the human race by our Savior, Jesus Christ. The homilist went on to speak of original sin—a topic that does not make many homilies today. As the *United States Catholic Catechism for Adults* states: "There is a perceptible discomfort in our culture with the notion of sin as an evil for which we must give an account to God, our Creator, Redeemer, and Judge" (*USCCA* 71).

Yet, through original sin, that devastating act of disobedience performed by our first parents, the human race was deprived of its pristine innocence, lost the grace with which it was endowed by its Creator from the beginning, and was separated from God by an eternal divide. The effects of that original sin, that Fall of man, have perdured down through the ages. The Catechism makes it clear that original sin is alive and well and cannot be eliminated from our Church teaching.

In fact, in the *United States Catholic Catechism for Adults*, speaking of the Fall of our first parents, we read: "The language is figurative, but the reality is not a fantasy" (*USCCA* 69). Original Sin is an essential truth of our faith. The Catechism points out, moreover, that "the doctrine of original sin is, so to speak, the 'reverse side' of the Good News"(*CCC* 389). We cannot tamper with the revelation of original sin without undermining the mystery of Christ—that Jesus lived, died, and rose precisely to undo the sin of Adam, to make it possible for us to live with God forever. Jesus is the new Adam and as such is Savior of the world.

The account of the Fall, of original sin, is found in Genesis 2 and 3. Although written in figurative language, it is nonetheless part of the revealed Word of God. In Genesis 2:17 God tested our first parents and forbade them to eat of "the tree of knowledge of good and bad . . . the moment you eat from it you are surely doomed to die." God placed limits on them; he still does on each of us. We all know how Adam and Eve disobeyed and ate from the fruit of the tree, the tree from which God had forbidden them to eat.

Tricked by the seductive voice of the devil, one of the fallen angels, the first sin, the original sin, was a sin of failure to trust God by disobeying his command. It was a lack of trust and disobedience. "In that sin man *preferred* himself to God and by that very act scorned him" (*CCC* 398). All subsequent sin is in effect disobedience of God and failure to trust in his goodness. What were the consequences of this first sin? Adam and Eve immediately lost the grace of sharing in God's life. The sense of innocence and harmony among body, passions, will, and mind was lost. Division, strife, domination, greed, suffering, and death entered into human history.

Since that first sin, the world has become virtually inundated by sin. Each of us, whether we understand it or not, lives with the consequences of original sin. Adam and Eve transmitted to their descendants a human nature wounded by

their own first sin. To this day, there is still an inner war within each of us between the spirit and the flesh (Gal 5:16–17).
Adam and Eve "committed a *personal sin*, but this sin affected
the *human nature* that they would then transmit *in a fallen state*
[Footnote: Cf. Council of Trent: *DS* 1511–1512]" (*CCC* 404).

Original sin, an expression coined by Saint Augustine, is a
sin "contracted" and not "committed." It is a "state" and not
an "act" (*CCC* 404). It is a deprivation of original holiness and
justice rather than a personal fault in any of Adam's descendants. We are born with the effects of original sin. It is manifested in our inclination to evil. That is our spiritual struggle,
a struggle to become holy. That is why the Church requires
Baptism. Baptism erases original sin, turns us back to God,
and incorporates us in the life of Christ. But the consequences
for nature—your nature and my nature, a weakened nature
and a nature inclined to evil—persist in each of us and sum-
mon us to spiritual battle. God did not leave us alone in this
battle. After the Fall, he did not abandon us. "In Jesus Christ,
we can overcome the power of sin, for it is the Lord's desire
that all come to salvation" (*USCCA* 72).

In the beautiful season of Advent, the Church expresses
her longing for the Christ who came into the world at his
birth, and we long for the Lord who will come at the end of
history. It is Jesus who is the Christmas answer to the Fall of
our first parents, Jesus born of parents, Mary and Joseph. Furthermore, it is Jesus, the new Adam, who in becoming obedient even unto death makes amends superabundantly for the
disobedience of Adam. The Catechism teaches that "the victory that Christ won over sin has given us greater blessings
than those which sin had taken from us: 'where sin increased,
grace abounded all the more'" (Rom 5:20; *CCC* 420).

In his classic book *Crossing the Threshold of Hope*, our late
Holy Father John Paul II speaks of the reality of sin, the exis-
tence of original sin, and the promise of salvation born in the
Christmas crib. In this context he writes:

Nevertheless, convincing the world of the existence of sin is not the same as condemning it for sinning. "God did not send his Son into the world to condemn the world, but that the world might be saved through him." *Convincing the world of sin means creating the conditions for its salvation.* Awareness of our own sinfulness, including that which is inherited, is the first condition for salvation; the next is the confession of this sin before God, who desires only to receive this confession so that He can save man. *To save means to embrace and lift up with redemptive love,* with love that is *always greater* than any sin.

Recently, I saw a "Come Home for Christmas" poster that read: "Peace in the world starts with peace in your heart." That peace takes hold within us when we turn to Jesus and seek the forgiveness of our sins, for this is why he came into the world.

Reflect

1. Reflect on these words of Pope Benedict XVI: "Faith does not just mean accepting a certain number of abstract truths about the mysteries of God, of man, of life and death, of future realities. . . . Believing means surrendering ourselves to God and entrusting our destiny to him . . . and making this relationship the basis of our whole life."

   How would you describe what faith means to you?

2. Our God is at once close at hand, present to us in the
    peace of our prayer and in sacramental encounters,
    and at the same time seemingly distant.

    In your recent experience, has God seemed close
    at hand or distant?

3. Reflect on these words from Gerald O'Collins,
    S.J., and Mary Venturini: "God is not a celluloid
    Superman who holds up crumbling dams, pastes
    back the earthquake cracks, forces missiles off their
    path, stops helicopters crashing to the ground and
    kills the terrible tyrant just in time to save mankind
    from disaster."

    How do you answer the question: Why do bad
    things happen to good people?

4. What were the consequences of this first sin? Adam
    and Eve immediately lost the grace of sharing in
    God's life. The sense of innocence and harmony
    among body, passions, will, and mind was lost.
    Division, strife, domination, greed, suffering, and
    death made their entrance into human history.

    Are there ways in which the Church's teaching
    about original sin helps me to make sense of my
    personal life or interactions with others?

5. What else in this chapter was important to you?

Pray

I arise today
through a mighty strength, the invocation of the Trinity,

through the belief in the threeness,
through confession of the oneness
of the Creator of Creation.

I arise today
through God's strength to pilot me:
God's might to uphold me,
God's wisdom to guide me,
God's eye to look before me,
God's ear to hear me,
God's word to speak for me,
God's hand to guard me,
God's way to lie before me,
God's shield to protect me,
God's host to save me
from snares of devils,
from temptations of vices,
from everyone who shall wish me ill,
afar and anear,
alone and in multitude.

I arise today
through a mighty strength, the invocation of the Trinity,
through belief in the threeness,

through confession of the oneness
of the Creator of Creation.

—From the Breastplate of Saint Patrick

TWO

I Believe in Jesus Christ, His Only Son, Our Lord

The second part of the Apostles' Creed focuses on our faith in Jesus. These christological articles (i.e., those dealing with Christ) make up the most substantial portion of the creed. This should not surprise us for "at the heart of catechesis we find, in essence, a Person, the Person of Jesus of Nazareth, the only Son from the Father . . . who suffered and died for us and who now, after rising, is living with us forever (CT 5)" (CCC 426). "Whoever has seen me has seen the Father," Jesus said to the apostle Philip (Jn 14:9). The first Preface of Christmas refers to Jesus in this way: "In him, we see our God made visible, and so are caught up in love of the God we cannot see."

Who is this Jesus? Pope Paul VI once said: "I can never cease to speak of Christ for he is our truth and our light" (USCCA 87). As Christians we are all called to say the same. We all have pinned our life and our very hope on Jesus. We see the world through "Christ-colored glasses."

There is a popular poem, written about a hundred years ago, that one occasionally sees in Christmas cards, "One Solitary Life."

He was born in an obscure village,
a child of a peasant woman.
He grew up in another obscure village
where he worked in a carpenter shop until he was thirty.
Then for three years

he was an itinerant preacher.
He never had a family or owned a home.
He never set foot inside a big city.
He never traveled two hundred miles from the place he was born.
He never wrote a book or held an office.
He did none of the things that usually accompany greatness.
While he was still a young man,
the tide of popular opinion turned against him.
His friends deserted him.
He was turned over to his enemies.
He went through the mockery of a trial.
He was nailed to a cross between two thieves.
While he was dying his executioners gambled
for the only piece of property he had, his coat.
When he was dead, he was taken down
and laid in a borrowed grave.
Nineteen centuries have come and gone
and today he is still the central figure
for much of the human race.
All the armies that ever marched,
all the navies that ever sailed,
all the parliaments that ever sat,
and all the kings that ever reigned,
put together, have not affected the life of man
upon this earth as powerfully as this
One Solitary Life.

It is for us not enough simply to understand the historical life of Jesus, as important as that is. "We ponder Christ's person and his earthly words and deeds in terms of *mystery*. His earthly life reveals his hidden divine Sonship and plan for our salvation" (*USCCA* 79). He preached the kingdom of heaven, the breaking through of God into our very life and existence every day. "The Kingdom of God is his presence among human beings calling them to a new way of life as individuals and as a community" (*USCCA* 79).

The Catechism explains that "catechesis aims at putting 'people . . . in communion . . . with Jesus Christ: only he can lead us to the love of the Father in the Spirit and make us share in the life of the Holy Trinity' (CT 5)" (CCC 426). The Jesus who now brings you and me into the new life of God is not merely the Jesus who once upon a time lived, died, and rose from the dead. His presence to us did not end with his resurrection and Ascension. The living Christ, in whom we believe and whom we constantly experience, and the historical Jesus are one and the same person. The Jesus of history is, after all, the Christ of faith.

During the Christmas season we encounter the living Lord as we celebrate his birth on Christmas Day. At the octave of Christmas (New Year's Day), we share with Mary in the ceremony of circumcision and, the official naming of her Son. At the Epiphany we celebrate him as the light for all people and remember his baptism, which reveals our call to share in his mission. So our faith is indeed a faith in the living Christ whom we encounter in the liturgy.

When we profess this baptismal faith in the creed, we express it in these four titles: Jesus, Christ, Son of God, Lord. What do they reveal about our God?

Jesus

In Hebrew, *Jesus* means "God saves." It was the angel at the Annunciation who told Mary that she would bear a son "and you shall name him Jesus" (Lk 1:31). His name reveals both his mission and his identity. His very name reveals his whole purpose—to save us. As Pope Benedict said in his Christmas homily in 2006, responding to the question whether modern man still needs a savior: ". . . In this post-modern age, perhaps he needs a Savior all the more, since the society in which he lives has become more complex and the threats to his personal and moral integrity have become more insidious." What is the object of salvation? It is to save us from our sins. Thus to speak of Jesus without understanding the linkage to sin is simply to miss his whole reason for becoming man. Because sin is always an offense against God, only God can forgive sin. In the New Testament, the term savior is applied only to God (eight times) or to Jesus (sixteen times). No one else is called "savior." The name of Jesus is at the heart of all Christian prayer. "Nor is there any other name under heaven given to the human race by which we are to be saved" (Acts 4:12).

Christit

Christ is not the last name of Jesus. No, he is Jesus, the Christ. *Christ* comes from the Greek translation of the Hebrew word for messiah. *Christ* means "the Anointed One." As you and I were anointed at Baptism, Jesus was anointed with the Holy Spirit at his baptism by John and sent "to bring glad tidings to the poor /. . . to proclaim liberty to captives / and recovery of sight to the blind, / to let the oppressed go free, / and to proclaim a year acceptable to the Lord" (Lk 4:18–19). Again, it was an angel who announced to the shepherds on Christmas Eve that Jesus was the Messiah, the Christ: "For today in the city of David a savior has been born for you who is Messiah and Lord" (Lk 2:11).

The Only Son of God

The gospels report that at two solemn moments, Christ's baptism and his transfiguration, the Father's voice designated Jesus as his "beloved Son." Jesus also called himself "the Son"

(Mt 11:27) and by this title affirmed his unique relationship to God his Father: He is the only Son of God. You and I are "adopted" sons and daughters of God, with our own adoption taking place when we were baptized.

Regarding the title Son of God, Gerald O'Collins and Mary Venturini write:

> In all their simplicity these few words contain the essence of Christianity, the point where Christians are forced to leave their Jewish heritage behind. It is just possible that the old covenant could have embraced Jesus the savior as the longed-for and long-heralded messiah. But there was no room for the Son of God. God, for the Jews then and now, was and is without form or physical substance. God could not therefore become man without revolutionizing the whole Jewish faith. That God should have a Son was folly enough; that the Son should take human form was madness; that he should be both man and God was blasphemy.

Lord

The Hebrew name *Yahweh* is translated *Kyrios* in Greek, which means "Lord." The title "Lord," used for both the Father and Jesus, indicates divine sovereignty. To confess or invoke Jesus as Lord is to believe in his divinity and bow our knee in worship of him (Phil 2:10–11). "No one can say, 'Jesus is Lord,' except by the holy Spirit" (1 Cor 12:3).

The prologue of John's gospel expresses the truth of the incarnation in this way: "The Word became flesh / and made his dwelling among us" (Jn 1:14). Why did the Word become flesh? Or, as Saint Anselm of Canterbury asked the question: *Cur Deus Homo*? Why did God become man? It is the quintessential Christmas question, and it is a question we often ignore or simply fail to ask. With the Nicene Creed, we answer by confessing: "For us men and for our salvation he came down from heaven: by the power of the Holy Spirit he was born of the Virgin Mary, and became man."

In a Christmas homily, I once sought to answer Anselm's question in the following way: "In a word, he came to pitch his tent among us, to be with us forever, to demonstrate our inestimable worth and dignity as humans, to feed us on his life, to save us out of love that we might forever be with him." The Son of God wanted to live among us, to show us just how uniquely valuable we are, to share his life with us and to bring us to our final home with him forever. I will always remember how John Paul II ended his Christmas homily a few years ago with the following words in Italian: "*Dio ci ama*" (God loves us). He pitched his tent among us, above all, because he loves us.

The Catechism gives us four reasons in answer to the "why" of the Incarnation:

1. "The Word became flesh for us *in order to save us by reconciling us with God*" (CCC 457), who "loved us and sent his Son as expiation for our sins" (1 Jn 4:10).

2. "The Word became flesh *so that thus we might know God's love*" (CCC 458), for "God so loved the world that he gave his only Son, so that everyone who believes in him might not perish but might have eternal life" (Jn 3:16).

3. "The Word became flesh *to be our model of holiness*" (CCC 459). "I am the way and the truth and the life. No one comes to the Father except through me" (Jn 14:6). Jesus is the norm of the

new law: "Love one another as I love you" (Jn 15:12).

4. "The Word became flesh to make us '*partakers of the divine nature*'" (*CCC* 460, cf. 2 Pt 1:4). Speaking of this "wondrous exchange," Saint Gregory of Nyssa (d. around 395) wrote: "God takes on the poverty of my flesh so that I may receive the riches of his godhead." He became man without ceasing to be God so that we might be divinized without ceasing to be human beings. In a certain sense, he united himself with each of us (*CCC* 457–460).

We speak of this mystery as the Incarnation, a word whose Latin root means "becoming flesh." Our faith teaches us: "The unique and altogether singular event of the Incarnation of the Son of God does not mean that Jesus Christ is part God and part man, nor does it imply that he is the result of a confused mixture of the divine and the human. He became truly man while remaining truly God. Jesus Christ is true God and true man" (*CCC* 464). During the first centuries the Church struggled to clarify this truth of faith against the heresies that falsified it. Some heretics affirmed Christ's divinity while denying his true humanity. According to Docetism, for example, he only appeared to be human. Other heretics such as Arius (d. around AD 336) and his followers denied that Jesus was truly divine and of "one being" with God the Father.

The Catechism follows the early councils of the Church by teaching clearly that Jesus' divine and human natures are inseparable. He is truly God and truly man. This teaching on Christ underlies our entire faith. In the words of the Council of Chalcedon (451): "We confess that one and the same Christ, Lord, and only-begotten Son, is to be acknowledged in two natures without confusion, change, division, or separation" (*CCC* 467).

The human nature of Christ was assumed, not absorbed. He worked with human hands, thought with a human mind, acted with a human will, and loved with a human heart (*GS* 22). He grew up physically and mentally, thought, made decisions, felt deep emotions, wept, ate, drank, entered into personal relationships, talked, suffered, and eventually died. These and further facts about him justify our recognizing him as fully human, even if he was virginally conceived. His conception through the Holy Spirit pointed to his personal identity as Son of God and showed that he was not and is not merely human. "The Incarnation is therefore the mystery of the wonderful union of the divine and human natures in the one person of the Word" (*CCC* 483). "Jesus Christ is the divine Son of God who became man in the womb of Mary. The one who was born of Mary is the same one—the same person— who has existed with the Father and the Holy Spirit from all eternity" (*USCCA* 82).

Reflect

1. We have pinned our life and very hope on Jesus.

    In what ways are these words true for you? In what ways are they not?

2. Christ worked with human hands, thought with a human mind, acted with a human will, and loved with a human heart. He grew up physically and mentally, thought, made decisions, felt deep emotions, wept, ate, drank, entered into personal relationships, talked, suffered, and eventually died.

    What aspect of Jesus' humanity is most important for you at this time in your life?

3.   What else in this chapter was important to you?

Pray

Radiating Christ

(A daily prayer used by late Mother Teresa and by the
Sisters of the Missionaries of Charity)

Dear Jesus,
help us to spread your fragrance everywhere we go.
Flood our souls with your spirit and life.
Penetrate and possess our whole being so utterly
that our lives may only be a radiance of yours.
Shine through us, and be so in us,
that every soul we come in contact with
may feel your presence in our soul.
Let them look up and see no longer us but only Jesus!
Stay with us, and then we shall begin to shine as you shine;
so to shine as to be a light to others;
the light O Jesus, will be all from you,
none of it will be ours;
it will be you, shining on others through us.
Let us thus praise you in the way you love best
by shining on those around us.
Let us preach you without preaching,
not by words but by our example,
by the catching force, the sympathetic influence of what
we do.
The evident fullness of the love our hearts bear to you.
Amen.

—Cardinal Newman

THREE

He Was Conceived by the Power of the Holy Spirit, and Born of the Virgin Mary

Like others, Cardinal Schönborn points out: ". . . the catechism does not treat Mary's role in the plan of salvation in a separate chapter. It does so here in the pages devoted to Christ, inasmuch as she enjoys the unique privilege of being the Mother of God." The Catechism says as much: "What the Catholic faith believes about Mary is based on what it believes about Christ, and what it teaches about Mary illumines in turn its faith in Christ" (CCC 487). She always leads us to him.

"The Holy Spirit, 'the Lord, the giver of Life,' is sent to sanctify the womb of the Virgin Mary and divinely fecundate it, causing her to conceive the eternal Son of the Father in a humanity drawn from her own" (CCC 485).

From all eternity, God chose for the mother of his Son a daughter of Israel, a young Jewish woman of Nazareth in Galilee, "a virgin betrothed to a man named Joseph, of the house of David, and the virgin's name was Mary" (Lk 1:27).

Through the centuries, the Church has become ever more aware that Mary, from the very first moment of her conception, was redeemed in a unique way through being filled with grace by God and thus preserved from any sin, even original sin. In the dogma of the Immaculate Conception, proclaimed in 1854, Pope Pius IX wrote that she was "preserved immune from all stain of original sin." The Church often speaks of Mary as the "Second Eve." Whereas the first Eve helped usher

death into the world, Mary ushered life into the world. And
she did so with the obedience of faith. As she said to God's
messenger, *"fiat voluntas tua"* (thy will be done) (Lk 1:26–38),
she gave herself entirely to the person and work of her Son.

Speaking on November 29, 2006, in Ephesus, where Tradition holds that Mary lived after Pentecost, Pope Benedict
taught beautifully:

> Mary's motherhood, which began with her *"fiat"*
> in Nazareth, is fulfilled at the foot of the Cross.
> Although it is true—as Saint Anselm says—that
> "from the moment of her *fiat* Mary began to carry
> all of us in her womb," the maternal vocation and
> mission of the Virgin towards those who believe
> in Christ actually began when Jesus said to her:
> "Woman, behold, your son!" (Jn 19:26) from the
> Cross.

In a thought-provoking homily on this section of the Catechism, Cardinal John O'Connor (d. 2000), the late archbishop
of New York, wrote:

> We must remember that Mary was invited to be-
> come the Mother of the Son of God. She was a vir-
> gin. She could have said, "I can't do this. It's going
> to be terribly inconvenient. What will Joseph say?
> What will my parents say?" She was invited. What
> would have happened if Mary had said no to the
> angel? Would there have been a Christmas, a cru-
> cifixion? Would we be here today? Doesn't the
> Holy Spirit say the same to every woman, to every
> couple whom He invites to bear the Child whose
> life can only come from God? "The Holy Spirit will
> come upon you. Do not be afraid."

Our faith teaches us that Jesus was conceived solely by the
power of the Holy Spirit and that Mary was ever virgin: real

and perpetual. Mary's virginity manifests God's absolute initiative in the Incarnation. Saint Augustine, writing of Mary's virginity but highlighting the preeminence of her faith, said: "Mary is more blessed because she embraces faith in Christ than because she conceives the flesh of Christ [Footnote: St. Augustine, *De virg.*, 3: *PL* 40, 398]" (*CCC* 506).

The Mystery of Christ's Life: Sacrament of His Divinity

For more than a century, historians and biblical scholars have explored in great detail the story of Jesus' life. They have scrutinized thoroughly all that the gospels record about what Jesus taught, did, and suffered.

The Catechism approaches the events of Christ's life from a different perspective—as religious "mysteries." The word *mystery* comes from the Greek *mysterion* (in Latin: *sacramentum*), which means a "secret revealed by God," a deeply important truth that has now been disclosed to guide and nourish our lives.

Like the gospels themselves, the Catechism seeks to communicate not some kind of "scientific" biography of Jesus, but the real meaning of the events and actions of his life that will nourish our faith. The four gospels came from individuals who were among the first to enjoy Christian faith, and they wanted to share that faith with others. The gospels were written "that you may [come to] believe that Jesus is the Messiah, the Son of God, and that through this belief you may have life in his name" (Jn 20:31).

> The whole of Christ's life was a continual teaching: his silences, his miracles, his gestures, his prayer, his love for people, his special affection for the little and the poor, his acceptance of the total sacrifice on the Cross for the redemption of

the world, and his Resurrection [Footnote: John
Paul II, *CT* 9]. . . . (*CCC* 561)

In pondering the life of Christ when we pray and when
we celebrate the sacraments, our question must always be:
What does this action of Jesus, this preference of Jesus, this
word of Jesus reveal and communicate to us about the Father,
about our God? In effect, what is the deep religious truth expressed by the birth of Jesus, his hidden life, his baptism, his
solitude and temptation in the desert, his miracles and signs,
the transfiguration, his death and Resurrection? This is no
mere intellectual exercise but something that touches our life
deeply.

We grow in Christ by identifying with the mysteries of
his public life, such as his baptism, the temptations he faced,
his preaching and witness to the kingdom. We are affected,
and transformed into him, experiencing ongoing redemption.
All Jesus did, said, and suffered had as its aim the restoration
of fallen humanity to its original vocation. Christ enables us,
here and now, to live in him, to live all that he lived. He lives
in us anew. As Saint Paul teaches: "Yet I live, no longer I, but
Christ lives in me" (Gal 2:20). He continually reveals himself
to us each and every day, transforming us in and through the
mystery of his whole life.

The sections in the Catechism on the life of Christ (*CCC*
522–570) and Chapter Seven of the *United States Catholic Catechism for Adults* are well worth reading and rereading. Jesus
is, after all, not just a past figure from history. He is the living
Christ of our faith today.

Reflect

1. Mary could have said, "I can't do this. It's going to be terribly inconvenient." But she said instead: "Thy will be done."

   In your life today, why is it sometimes difficult for you to say yes to God?

2. Reflect on Cardinal O'Connor's question: "What would have happened if Mary had said no to the angel?"

   How has saying yes to God changed your life?

3. What else in this chapter was important to you?

Pray

Loving Mother of the Redeemer,
gate of heaven,
star of the sea,
assist your people who have fallen yet strive to rise again.
To the wonderment of nature you bore your Creator,
yet remained a virgin after as before!
You who received Gabriel's joyful greeting,
have pity on us poor sinners.

—From the Liturgy of the Hours

FOUR

He Suffered Under Pontius Pilate, Was Crucified, Died, and Was Buried

Out of love for each of us Jesus Christ "suffered under Pontius Pilate, was crucified, died, and was buried." In this fourth article of the Apostles' Creed, Jesus continues to reveal himself to us not only by his words but also by his deeds and signs. Through words and deeds he communicated who he was and is, and completed and perfected revelation. But "above all," in the words of the Vatican Council II's *Dogmatic Constitution on Divine Revelation,* he revealed himself "by His death and glorious resurrection from the dead" (*DV* 4). Stated differently, in the words of the Catechism, the Paschal Mystery (his Cross and Resurrection) "stands at the center of the Good News that the apostles, and the Church following them, are to proclaim to the world" (*CCC* 571). In this section we focus on the integral place of Jesus' suffering and death in the mystery of Christ and his redemption—out of love—for each of us. "God's saving plan was accomplished 'once for all' (Heb 9:26) by the redemptive death of his Son Jesus Christ" (*CCC* 571). As Archbishop Donald W. Wuerl writes: "Nothing of Christian life can be understood apart from the cross. By his cross we are saved and brought to life."

Suffered Under Pontius Pilate

The Creed is very specific in this matter. Pilate was the Roman governor of Judea from AD 26 to 36. His name in the Creed fixes precisely the particular time and place in human history of Jesus' suffering. It attests to its historical reality and its integral role for our faith. The name of Pilate also conjures up the climax of Jesus' suffering—his death on the Cross.

From the gospels, we know the horrifying details of Christ's suffering: agony in the garden, the scourging, the crowning with thorns, the carrying of the Cross, and ultimately the horrible death by crucifixion.

Christian devotion has helped us focus prayerfully on the suffering of Christ—the five Sorrowful Mysteries of the Rosary, the fourteen Stations of the Cross, and the Seven Last Words of Jesus. The latter two devotions are encouraged in a special fashion during the holy season of Lent.

As we begin this section, I invite you to listen to the moving words of Jesus from the Cross. It is his prayer from the Cross. These words of prayer come from the depth of his soul and express his great love for us. They are recorded in the four gospels. In effect, there are seven sets of words:

1. "Father, forgive them, they know not what they do" (Lk 23:34).

2. "Amen, I say to you, today you will be with me in Paradise" (Lk 23:43).

3. "Woman, behold, your son. . . . Behold, your mother" (Jn 19:26–27).

4. "My God, my God, why have you forsaken me?" (Mk 15:34).

5. "I thirst" (Jn 19:28).

6. "It is finished" (Jn 19:30).

7. "Father, into your hands I commend my
   spirit." (Lk 23:46).

If we listen closely from the depth of our hearts, we can perceive a privileged glimpse of the boundless depth of Jesus' prayer to his Father and our Father. Jesus speaks and acts from the pulpit of the Cross. Jesus speaks precisely through his terrible pain and suffering, through his crucifixion, which is the supreme act of unselfish love. This is the climactic deed of his whole life. His words on the Cross are uttered in agony, but they are also his prayer. It is acting and speaking coming together in a dramatic way. He acted out his teaching. As we stand by that Cross and listen, we then make his prayer, his words, our own.

His words are akin to a spiritual commentary on what he was doing for us. His words give lasting credibility to his magnificent act of love for us. This act gives a credible and meaningful context to his words, these last words that he uttered from the pulpit of the Cross. They are words of prayer, drawn in part from the Hebrew psalms, words of communion with his Father, words of communion and solidarity with and for others to hear, words for us to hear over and over again. They inspire us to greater faith and reverence for the saving power of our God. If the agony on the Cross had not happened, if his heart had not been pierced, it would be extremely difficult to believe the truth that God is love.

For Jesus did not simply speak of suffering or offer an explanation about it. No, he embraced it, accepted it, shared it, and transformed it out of love for us.

By accomplishing our redemption precisely in and through suffering, Christ has raised human suffering, all human suffering—every aspect and dimension of our human suffering—to the level of our redemption (SD 19). He has given suffering a new meaning. The mystery of human suffering now has a salvific meaning. Each one of us can thus see in our suffering and in the suffering of others the face of

Christ Jesus. It is in suffering where we meet him personally and where we touch and experience his saving power. In his book with Mary Venturini, Gerald O'Collins writes:

> I shrink from giving the impression of glorifying pain and wallowing in suffering. But "he suffered under Pontius Pilate" applies to all of us. There is always some Pontius Pilate around to put pain into our lives. No matter who we are, we cannot avoid the cross. The choice is simple. We can curse the pain. Or we can lay it at the feet of Jesus. If we do that, we will know our pain and our lives to be transformed. . . . Murder or some other fierce tragedy can unexpectedly bring the cross into our lives. Or else our particular Pontius Pilate may turn up in a less dramatic fashion. Either way we all constantly face the challenge: Do we keep our eyes down and curse our cross? Or do we lift our gaze and link our pain with our unique fellow sufferer, the Son of God himself?

The Catechism speaks of the "why" of Jesus' suffering and Death. Already "from the beginning of Jesus' public ministry, certain Pharisees and partisans of Herod together with priests and scribes agreed together to destroy him (cf. Mk 3:6; 14:1)" (CCC 574), as if he were a marked man. At the beginning of his gospel, Mark says it succinctly: "The Pharisees went out and immediately took counsel with the Herodians against him to put him to death" (Mk 3:6). Moreover, Jesus predicted on multiple occasions his passion. Pain and death would be an essential part of his mission. "Not only would Jesus accept the Cross, he expected the same willingness from his disciples. 'If anyone wishes to come after me, he must deny himself, take up his cross daily and follow me'" (Lk 9:23, USCCA 91).

Why would Jesus suffer and die? The Catechism gives the following reasons: "Because of certain of his acts—expelling demons, forgiving sins, healing on the sabbath day . . . his familiarity with tax collectors and public sinners (Cf. Mt 12:24; Mk 2:7, 14–17; 3:1–6; 7:14–23)—some ill-intentioned persons suspected Jesus of demonic possession (Cf. Mk 3:22; Jn 8:48; 10:20). He is accused of blasphemy and false prophecy, religious crimes which the Law punished with death by stoning (Cf. Mk 2:7; Jn 5:18; Jn 7:12; 7:52; 8:59; 10:31, 33)" (CCC 574).

There are also other reasons. The Catechism makes it clear that "in the eyes of many in Israel," Jesus seemed to be acting against three essential institutions of the Chosen People: the Law, the Temple, and Israel's belief in one God and savior.

Jesus and the Law

"Do not think that I have come to abolish the law or the prophets. I have come not to abolish but to fulfill" (Mt 5:17). These are words spoken by Jesus early in his Sermon on the Mount. Despite that reassurance, he could not help but offend the teachers of the Law. Jesus spoke with authority about the Law, and his interpretation was different from theirs. "You have heard it said . . . but I say to you," he would say emphatically. To "fulfill" the Law means to go beyond the Law, to refine and transform it, to lead it to perfection.

Jesus and the Temple

Forty days after his birth, we celebrate the Presentation of the Lord in the Temple. Following Jewish practice, Mary and Joseph would have brought Jesus to the Temple at this time. Like the prophets, Jesus always expressed deepest respect for the Temple in Jerusalem. For him, it was a house of prayer, the dwelling place of God, and he visited it annually for the major Jewish feasts. On the threshold of his passion, however, Jesus announced the coming destruction of the Temple (which did happen in AD 70). By saying this he meant to foreshadow his own death and resurrection. His body would become the definitive Temple. But this prophecy would be distorted in its telling by false witnesses during his interrogation at the high priest's house, and would be thrown back at him as an insult when he was nailed to the Cross.

One can understand how offensive Jesus' language about the Temple proved to be. The wonderful Temple in Jerusalem was the great sign of God's presence and the focal point for Jewish religious life. Here was Jesus announcing that the Temple would be destroyed and would be replaced by a new relationship with God, a new Temple "not made with hands" (Mk 14:58).

Israel's Faith in One God and Savior

"Jesus performed acts, such as pardoning sins, that manifested him to be the Savior God himself (cf. Jn 5:16–18). Certain Jews, who did not recognize God made man (cf. Jn 1:14), saw in him only a man who made himself God (Jn 10:33), and judged him as a blasphemer" (CCC 594). By forgiving sins in his own name Jesus put himself on a par with God. This was to challenge the Jewish faith that made no room for any personal distinction between Father and Son.

Was Crucified, Died, and Was Buried

In talking about the crucifixion, the Catechism is quite clear from the outset that the Jews are not collectively responsible for the death of Jesus. "We cannot lay responsibility for the trial on the Jews in Jerusalem as a whole. . . . Still less can we extend responsibility to other Jews of different times and places" (CCC 597).

The *United States Catholic Catechism for Adults*, citing *Nostra Aetate* and the Catechism, adds: "Neither all Jews indiscriminately at that time, nor Jews today, can be charged with the crimes committed during his Passion. . . . The Jews should not be spoken of as rejected or accursed as if this followed from holy Scripture" (*USCCA* 93).

The Catechism clearly states: "The Church has never forgotten that 'sinners were the authors and the ministers of all the sufferings that the divine Redeemer endured' [Footnote: *Roman Catechism* I, 5, 11; cf. Heb 12:3]" (*CCC* 598). Even the prayers that the Church uses on Good Friday have been changed to remind us that the sins of each of us are responsible for the death of Jesus.

The Catechism quotes Saint Francis of Assisi about this: "Since our sins made the Lord Christ suffer the torment of the cross, those who plunge themselves into disorders and crimes crucify the Son of God anew in their hearts (for he is in them) and hold him up to contempt [Footnote: *Roman Catechism* I, 5, 11; cf. Heb 6:6; 1 Cor 2:8]" (*CCC* 598). That means you and I, each one of us without exception, each one of us who sins and lives a life of sin, is responsible for Jesus' death.

Jesus' crucifixion, moreover, was not some random event that simply escaped the Father's care for his Son. No, it was decreed from all eternity. It was predestined from all time. It was the ultimate act of mercy and love for each of us. We can never forget this truth of our faith. It is worth pondering often in our prayer. The death of Jesus for our sins was "in accordance with the scriptures" (1 Cor 15:3). It was the way in which the Son would give human expression to the divine and eternal love Jesus has for the Father. "This is why the Father loves me, because I lay down my life," says the Lord, "but the world must know that I love the Father and that I do just as the Father has commanded me" (Jn 10:17, 14:31).

"His redemptive passion was the very reason for his Incarnation" (*CCC* 607), a total act of generous self-giving. Archbishop Donald W. Wuerl writes: "From the beginning the Church focused her attention on the infinite love that shines from the Cross of Christ. 'We preach Christ crucified' (1 Cor 1:23). 'Far be it from me to glory in the cross of our Lord Jesus Christ' (Gal 6:14). When the Gospels were written, the longest single section of each was the history of the passion."

By his death, Jesus assumed a solidarity with each of us, each of us sinners. In a mysterious way, he so identified with us, those he came to save, that God the Father "made him to be sin who did not know sin, so that we might become the righteousness of God in him" (2 Cor 5:21). He was not a passive victim. On the contrary, he offered himself to the Father for our sins. All of us can join Saint Paul in saying, "The Son of God . . . has loved me and given himself up for me" (Gal 2:20).

The crucifixion is that singular event in history by which, through the blood of the Cross, the whole of humanity was reconciled to God—that supreme act of love in which Jesus Christ gave his whole life over to the Father freely out of love for us and him. "No one takes [my life] from me, but I lay it down on my own" (Jn 10:18). "In the words of Christian Tradition, Jesus' sacrifice merits salvation for us because it retains forever the power to draw us to him and to the Father" (*USCCA* 92).

During the Last Supper, Jesus entered into his unique and definitive sacrifice, which would be completed by his death, Resurrection, and glorious Ascension into heaven. Remember his words: "This is my body, which will be given for you" (Lk 22:19). The paschal sacrifice is now fulfilled to be mysteriously made present again each time that we gather to celebrate the Eucharist. It is at the heart of our faith. That is why regular participation at the most holy Eucharist is essential in the life of a Christian. There should never be a Sunday when we without grave reason miss Mass, and we should attempt regularly to participate at Mass during the week if possible.

That Jesus' death is the perfect sacrifice of the new covenant, which he offered for all, and that it is an expiatory sacrifice are truths of the faith. Though both his soul and body remained united to the divine Word, Jesus truly died and was buried. It was from the tomb that he will arise to a newness of life that we experience every day of our lives if we only turn to him and repent for our sins.

Yes, it was out of love for us, that we can understand the fundamental vision of our faith that points beyond the ignominy of the Cross. The supreme clue of Calvary is love, not some softly sentimental love, a Valentine-card type of love, but a love that can move and change human hearts in a world where true caring and real compassion seem at times a lost art.

As we conclude this section, meditate with me on the *Pietà*, the dead Christ in the loving embrace of his sorrowful mother, who is our sorrowful mother too. I think of the beautiful statue in Saint Peter's Basilica. I have often visited it in Rome. There is a replica at historic Saint Patrick's Church in downtown Washington, D.C., and in many other churches. Twice someone tried to destroy the original in Rome. Both times it was fixed. At a more profound level, the mystery that the artistic creation represents can never be destroyed no matter how often one might try. The world tries repeatedly to eradicate this Jesus who died and suffered for us, but to no avail. The *Pietà* tells us so much about Jesus, about his loving mother Mary, and about ourselves.

That image challenges each of us, without exception, to see in the mystery of Christ's suffering and death the key to the mystery of our own daily suffering and ultimately to our death. By uniting himself to each of us in our suffering and death, Jesus gave meaning to the mystery of suffering, and he invites us to join our daily suffering to him who raises it to the supreme level of our sanctification and life forever with him. In the words of Saint Rose of Lima: "Apart from the cross there is no other ladder by which we may get to heaven [Footnote: St. Rose of Lima, cf. P. Hansen, *Vita mirabilis* (Louvain, 1668)]" (*CCC* 618).

As a practical reminder, we can not forget that the sacrament of the Anointing of the Sick provides those who are ill with a real way of uniting their sufferings with those of Christ. "By the grace of this sacrament the sick person receives the strength and the gift of uniting himself more closely to Christ's Passion: in a certain way he is consecrated to bear fruit by configuration to the Savior's redemptive Passion. Suffering, a consequence of original sin, acquires a new meaning; it becomes a participation in the saving work of Jesus" (*CCC* 1521).

Hopefully we will begin to see, little by little each day, that hidden in the crosses of our own sufferings is the seed of new life, risen life with the Lord. He had to suffer and die before he could rise again in glory. It is no different for you and me in Lent and beyond the Lenten season. That is the supreme paradox of the Christian life.

Reflect

1. Jesus did not simply speak of suffering or offer an explanation about it. No, he embraced it, accepted it, shared it, and transformed it out of love for us.

    How does the knowledge of the Cross change your experience of suffering?

    How does it affect the way you look at others' sufferings?

2. Reflect on Jesus' words:

    A hired man, who is not a shepherd and whose sheep are not his own, sees a wolf coming and leaves the sheep and runs away, and the wolf catches and scatters them. This is because he works for pay and has no concern for the sheep. I am the good shepherd, and I know mine and mine know me, just as the Father knows me and I know the Father; and I will lay down my life for the sheep (Jn 10:12–15).

What words, phrases, or images from this gospel passage resonate with your experience at this time?

3.   What else in this chapter was important to you?

Pray

Abroad the Regal Banners fly,
Now shines the Cross's mystery;
Upon it Life did death endure,
And yet by death did life procure.
Who, wounded with a direful spear,
Did, purposely to wash us clear
From stain of sin, pour out a flood
Of precious Water mixed with Blood.
That which the Prophet-King of old
Hath in mysterious verse foretold,
Is now accomplished, whilst we see
God ruling nations from a Tree.
O lovely and refulgent Tree,
Adorned with purpled majesty;
Culled from a worthy stock, to bear
Those Limbs which sanctified were.
Blest Tree, whose happy branches bore
The wealth that did the world restore;

The beam that did that Body weigh
Which raised up hell's expected prey.
Hail, Cross, of hopes the most sublime!
Now in this mournful Passion time,
Improve religious souls in grace,
The sins of criminals efface.
Blest Trinity, salvation's spring,
May every soul Thy praises sing;
To those Thou grantest conquest by
The holy Cross, rewards apply.

—A Medieval Hymn

FIVE

He Descended Into Hell.
On the Third Day He Rose Again

The late, well-known, and respected Jesuit Walter Burghardt once said in a homily, apropos of Lent,

> It is a journey that mingles gladness and sadness, satisfaction and frustration, high hopes and sometimes near despair. On the other hand, you walk that dusty journey with Jesus, and you walk it as risen Christians. You don't wait for Easter to rise with Christ; you don't wait for your very last death. You have risen! From the moment that water flowed over your forehead in the shape of a cross, the life of the risen Christ has been thrilling through your dust like another bloodstream.

We are always, even in Lent, risen Christians.

When we celebrate the mystery of the dramatic tragedy of Holy Week, we know the outcome already. The conclusion is revealed to us even as we begin this solemn week. Not only does Jesus, the central figure, die an ignominious death, but we know that through the power of God he miraculously rises from the dead three days later. When we celebrate the great events of our faith we are not simply remembering a past historical event. That historical event affects us significantly today and every day in our life. "When we speak of the Paschal Mystery, we refer to Christ's death and Resurrection as one inseparable event" (*USCCA* 93). By our Baptism, moreover, each of us, you and I, are configured to Christ in his dying and rising. Saint Paul teaches us that "always carrying about in the body the dying of Jesus, so that the life of Jesus may also be manifested in our body" (2 Cor 4:10). Our individual lives thus share—at this very moment and at every moment—in the very dying and rising of Jesus, in *his* Paschal Mystery. It rests at the very heart of Christian faith.

He Descended Into Hell

The Apostles' Creed confesses that Christ "descended into hell." "By the expression, 'He descended into hell,' the Apostles' Creed confesses that Jesus did really die and through his death for us conquered death and the devil 'who has the power of death'" (Heb 2:14, CCC 636). Thus, this article of the Creed reminds us, first of all, that Jesus truly died. His human story came to a dead stop. With Jesus' death, there is a solidarity with all men and women of all places and times both in the past and in the future—a radical solidarity with us even in our death. No matter how antiseptic, streamlined, packaged, and expensive modern death has become, none of us can put off death forever. Nor would Jesus.

In their book on the Creed, O'Collins and Venturini write these hope-filled words: "But in front of death we are faced with the great unknown, armed not with experience or reason but with the belief based on trust that Jesus Christ has gone before us not only through life but also through death." In fact, it is precisely through his death that Jesus brings salvation. By truly dying, Jesus changed the nature of death forever. He raised suffering and death to the level of our redemption.

In an artistic way, Eastern icons help us see a deeper dimension of the truth of Christ's descent. In icons, we often see Jesus delivering Adam and Eve, the patriarchs and their wives, John the Baptist, and others. Jesus' descent among the dead signals his liberation from the dead of all those who had died before him. He opened the gates of heaven for the just. "Christ went down into the depths of death so that 'the dead will hear the voice of the Son of God, and those who hear will live' (Jn 5:25; cf. Mt 12:40; Rom 10:7; Eph 4:9)" (*CCC* 635). He really died; he "conquered death and the devil," and his death had significance for all humanity.

The Catechism quotes a beautiful passage from an ancient homily by an unknown writer about Holy Saturday. It beautifully sums up Christ's descent into hell:

> Today a great silence reigns on earth, a great silence and a great stillness. A great silence because the King is asleep. The earth trembled and is still because God has fallen asleep in the flesh and he has raised up all who have slept ever since the world began. . . . He has gone to search for Adam, our first father, as for a lost sheep. Greatly desiring to visit those who live in darkness and in the shadow of death, he has gone to free from sorrow Adam in his bonds and Eve, captive with him— He who is both their God and the son of Eve . . . "I am your God, who for your sake have become your son . . . I order you, O sleeper, to awake. I did not create you to be a prisoner in hell. Rise from the dead, for I am the life of the dead." (*CCC* 635)

On the Third Day He Rose Again

In their joint book O'Collins and Venturini offer a profound insight about this article of the Creed: "Both then and now Christian faith stands or falls with the resurrection of Jesus from the dead. It was this unique piece of good news which got Christianity going and keeps it going." The Catechism calls it the "crowning truth of our faith in Christ" (*CCC*

638). It is a truth believed and lived by the first Christians. "Some of them even died as martyrs rather than deny what they had witnessed" (*USCCA* 95). It is a truth handed down in the Tradition. It is a truth set forth in scripture and later preached as an essential part of the Paschal Mystery. It has consequences even now for each baptized Christian. In short, our belief in Jesus' Resurrection is the basis for hope in our own. "If I go and prepare a place for you, I will come back again and take you to myself, so that where I am you also may be" (Jn 14:3).

The Catechism treats the Resurrection as both a "historical" and "transcendent" event. The first Christians were distinguished by their conviction that history now contained an incredible event. How did they know that the Jesus who walked with them along the dusty roads of Palestine had now been raised up? The first sign was the empty tomb. It is the gospel we read every Easter Sunday. The discovery of the empty tomb had significance for their Easter faith, just as it does for us. Moreover, by itself, even the empty tomb is not proof positive of the resurrection. After all, there were no eyewitnesses to his actual rising from the dead. The empty tomb is an important sign, a powerful sign. It signifies and gives meaning to the reality of the resurrection. But that meaning is supported and fleshed out by the post-resurrection appearances of the risen Lord. He was seen not by all, but by "the witnesses chosen by God in advance, who ate and drank with him after he rose from the dead" (Acts 10:41). These accounts of the appearance of the risen Jesus are the texts we hear each year during the Easter season at Mass.

Between Good Friday, when his disciples abandoned him, and Easter Sunday, when they became his witnesses, something had to have happened. There was an incredible encounter that changed their lives. And it was an initiative that came not from the disciples but from Christ, who was and is alive.

At the same time, the gospel image of the "empty tomb" can support, stimulate, and deepen our Easter faith. What does it mean for us and for the risen one? On Easter Sunday, the focus of the entire Christian world is an empty tomb. We listen and observe in the gospel reading for Easter Sunday from Saint John that Peter and John ran together to the tomb only to find it empty. Yes, an empty tomb! A powerful and important sign of hope and joy!

Reflect on three points about this empty tomb: First, through the eyes of faith—as believers—we know instinctively that what was not found there is alive within each of us. I speak of a person, a person with a face and voice. I speak of the risen Lord. That is our faith. In the great sacrament of Baptism, each of us was transformed as Jesus himself was transformed in the power of the resurrection. It is the risen Lord who lives within each of us. Saint Paul says: "I have been crucified with Christ; yet I live, no longer I, but Christ lives in me" (Gal 2:19–20).

The very emptiness of the tomb suggests and symbolizes the fullness of the new and everlasting life into which Jesus himself has gone. Graves naturally symbolize death and the end of life. The open and empty tomb of Jesus expresses the reversal of death and the start of a new life that will never end, the life of the risen one within each of us. When we look at ourselves in the mirror, we should be able to see the risen face of Jesus.

Second, the empty tomb is God's radical sign that redemption is not an escape from the suffering and death of this world to a better world. Instead, the empty tomb is an affirmation by God of this very world, a world in which we live and breathe and have our being. God did not discard Jesus' earthly corpse, but mysteriously raised and transfigured it. Unlike the case of Lazarus, Christ's resurrection was not merely a return to earthly life. Christ's resurrection is essentially different. The scriptures attest to the way the risen

Lord had been changed and transformed. Closed doors are no obstacle to him. He appears and disappears at will. People who have known him during his earthly existence fail, at least initially, to recognize him as the Jesus they knew. The scriptures attest to the way the risen Lord had been changed and transformed. This theme of transformation is found in all of the appearance accounts from the gospel readings each year during Easter week.

The empty tomb represents a transformation of our own material and bodily world. We see it very specifically in our lives when our sins are forgiven and we are reconciled to God and others. Just before Ash Wednesday, on February 19, 2007, Pope Benedict spoke these encouraging words about confession: "How many penitents find in confession the peace and joy they were seeking for so long!" Yes, a newness and transformation take place within us through the words of forgiveness. During Lent, we pray that large numbers of penitents will experience real transformation through the healing sacrament of Penance. We see the effect of this transformation when we experience with fresh eyes the liberating power of our lived Catholic faith. In effect, when a person comes from the cleansing sacrament of Penance, one can see the face of the risen Christ. Through the mystery of grace, he can and does change our present lives—even radically.

Third and finally, we often worry and ask ourselves: Who will roll back that large stone from the tombs of our lives? So many things in life seem impossible—the sufferings with which we struggle, the heavy burden of our sins that at times makes it impossible to see clearly, the injustices that we simply cannot forgive or endure. But God continues to do the impossible. He rolls away the enormous stones from our lives just as he rolled away the very large stone from the tomb of Jesus on that first Easter. He continues to let the light of Jesus' risen life into our concrete human circumstances. Every time we experience the living presence of the Lord, especially when we receive him in the Eucharist, it is as if a huge stone has been rolled back. It is then and there that we see the face of the risen Lord. It is the risen Lord, after all, whom we receive in Holy Communion. We see then with Easter eyes, and we know for sure that the Lord Jesus lives.

When reflecting on the resurrection, the Catechism also teaches that the resurrection is mysteriously the work of the entire Trinity. The Father's power raised Christ his Son. Saint Paul emphasizes the manifestation of God's power by the working of the Holy Spirit. "As for the Son, he effects his own Resurrection by virtue of his divine power. Jesus announces that the Son of man will have to suffer much, die, and then rise (Cf. Mk 8:31; 9:9–31; 10:34). Elsewhere he affirms explicitly: 'I lay down my life, that I may take it again. . . . I have power to lay it down, and I have power to take it again'" (Jn 10:17–18, CCC 649).

The Catechism adds a further point: "The Resurrection above all constitutes the confirmation of all Christ's works and teachings" (CCC 651). It has great implications for us. It is the basis of our hope. It pushes us beyond the threshold of hope. "If Christ has not been raised, then empty [too] is our preaching; empty, too, your faith" (1 Cor 15:14). The Paschal Mystery has two aspects that we must never forget: first, by his death, Christ liberates us from sin, and second, by his resurrection, he opens for us the way to a new life. The risen Christ lives in our hearts. In Christ, we have already tasted the powers of the age to come. What a wonderful perspective from which to approach Lent each year, the season when we intensively prepare ourselves to celebrate the Easter mystery, the very foundation of our faith.

Reflect

1. In front of death we are faced with the great unknown, armed not with experience or reason, but with the belief based on trust that Jesus Christ has gone before us, not only through life but also through death.

    Have you ever experienced the truth of these words in your own life or in the life of another? How would you describe that experience?

2. Between Good Friday, when his disciples abandoned him, and Easter Sunday, when they became his witnesses, something had to have happened. There was an incredible encounter that changed their lives.

    Why do you believe in Jesus' Resurrection?

3. What else in this chapter was important to you?

Pray

Have among yourselves the same attitude that is also yours in Christ Jesus,
Who, though he was in the form of God,
did not regard equality with God something to be grasped.
Rather, he emptied himself,
taking the form of a slave,
coming in human likeness;
and found human in appearance,
he humbled himself,
becoming obedient to death,
even death on a cross.

Because of this, God greatly exalted him
and bestowed on him the name
that is above every name,
that at the name of Jesus
every knee should bend,
of those in heaven and on earth and under the earth,
and every tongue confess that
Jesus Christ is Lord,
to the glory of God the Father.

—Philippians 2:5–11

SIX

He Ascended Into Heaven, and Is Seated at the Right Hand of the Father

The Ascension of our Lord is certainly overshadowed by the crucifixion and resurrection on the one side and Pentecost on the other. It seems almost unimportant. It takes up only a few lines in the Gospel of Luke (24:50–53), followed by a second flowery description in Acts (Acts 1:9–11). It has none of the tragedy of a final farewell, none of the agony and uncertainty of the Last Supper.

Yet how essential to our faith it is! Someone once described the Ascension as the grand Amen to a Bach cantata. It is a summation or capstone. It is the irreversible entry of Christ's humanity into divine glory symbolized by the cloud and by heaven, where he is now seated at the place of honor, at the right hand of the Father. Only the One who "came from the Father" can return to the Father. "Jesus Christ, the head of the Church, precedes us into the Father's glorious kingdom so that we, the members of his Body, may live in the hope of one day being with him for ever" (CCC 666).

What does this mean that Jesus was lifted up to heaven and is seated at the right hand of the Father? Although God has neither a right or left hand, there is a deep theological meaning to this. With the Ascension, and in Christ, human nature—the humanity we all share—has entered into the inner life of God in a new and hitherto unheard-of way. He now looks at us in eternity with the face of a man—Jesus. What great cause for hope!

By his Ascension the risen Jesus entered fully—with his humanity—into his share of divine glory. Heaven, after all, is not a place beyond the stars. It means that we now have a place in God. Where he has gone before us in glory, we hope to follow. He has preceded us to our eternal home in order to make sure that where he is, we, the members of his living Body, may also be.

By his Ascension Jesus did not disappear. Nor did he leave his apostles or us as orphans without a clear mission. Precisely in his leave-taking, he gave his followers a specific challenge. The Acts of the Apostles tells us that right before he left them he said to his apostles: "You will be my witnesses in Jerusalem . . . and to the ends of the earth" (Acts 1:8).

The duty to give witness, to proclaim the liberating truth about the Lord Jesus, also belongs to you and me. It calls for courageous witness. The Ascension is not simply a celebration of the exaltation of Jesus Christ, as significant as that is. It is also a clear reminder that the Lord wants a new kind of commitment from us, members of his living Body, the Church. The solemnity of the Ascension reminds us of the great and perennial challenge to go forth in witness of the Easter event. It is the same event that the apostles had experienced personally and that we continue to experience in the power of the Holy Spirit—that Christ is risen and lives. Alleluia, alleluia! The Ascension is an Easter feast.

Witness to the gospel, and integrally to the claims of social justice, is not optional for those of us who bear the name Christian. In fact the Church teaches that "Action on behalf of justice and participation in the transformation of the world fully appear to us as a *constitutive* dimension of the preaching of the Gospel. . . ." Works on behalf of the poor and the needy, another way to describe "preaching of the Gospel," are not just footnotes but an essential dimension to Christian witness.

At our parish school of the Little Flower in Bethesda, Maryland, from the earliest age, our children are introduced to their need to share what they have, to witness love, for those less fortunate. Eighth-grade students, for example, are engaged in outreach projects to help the poor and elderly as a required part of their preparation for Confirmation. This is an example of the witness Jesus had in mind before his leave-taking at the Ascension. In our witness of love, his presence remains even after he ascended into heaven.

I am personally very impressed by the many lawyers and doctors who give freely of their time and talents in pro-bono representation and care for the poor and needy. This is gener-ous witness to our life-giving faith. Many of those I know are members of the John Carroll Society, a group of professional and business men and women based in the Archdiocese of Washington. There is also a group of doctors and committed volunteers from the Washington, D.C., area who travel twice annually to a rural area of the Dominican Republic to care for the medical needs of the poorest of the poor. Is this outreach not constitutive of the gospel?

The annual March for Life and the many continuing ef-forts on behalf of the unborn and frail elderly are also public witnesses to the precious value of human life and witness to the very reason Jesus became man to take on our human flesh and raise it to the dignity of his life. What a profound witness, in our day, to the living practice of the faith!

There are so many examples in our nation of committed Christians, especially in our parishes, infused with a religious spirit who daily give witness to the faith "to the ends of the earth." In addition, many politicians struggle to reflect in their public positions aspects of our faith and gospel values. Ours, after all, is a faith revealed by Jesus Christ himself, who is "the way, the truth, and the life." Witness on his behalf is a wit-ness that gives renewed authenticity to all that we hold and believe, a faith protected by the truth that is the very person of Jesus Christ, the same Jesus who ascended into heaven but left us as his daily witnesses.

He did not leave the apostles alone. Nor does he leave us alone. He is still with us, and we are in and with him. In the marvelous words of Saint Augustine: "While in heaven, he is also with us; and we while on earth are with him."

Our risen and ascended Lord Jesus Christ is indeed with us always and in no more important way than in his very own Body and Blood—a pledge of eternal glory. In his apostolic letter on the Eucharist, *The Sacrament of Charity*, our Holy Father Benedict XVI writes: "Awakened by the preaching of God's word, faith is nourished and grows in the grace-filled encounter with the Risen Lord which takes place [in the Eucharist]" (*SC* 6).

Having entered the sanctuary of heaven once and for all, Jesus Christ, seated at the right hand of the Father, intercedes for us constantly. "Therefore, he is always able to save those who approach God through him, since he lives forever to make intercession for them" (Heb 7:25). The Messiah's kingdom is inaugurated. He is the unique mediator between us and God; exalted, in his glorified humanity, he assures us of the permanent outpouring of the Holy Spirit. "For there is one God. / There is also one mediator between God and / the human race, / Christ Jesus . . ." (1 Tim 2:5). What confidence this mystery of our faith, this sixth article of the Apostles' Creed, should inspire!

Reflect

1. With the Ascension, and in Christ, human nature—the humanity we all share—has entered into the inner life of God in a new and hitherto unheard-of way. He now looks at us in eternity with the face of a man, Jesus.

What words or phrases in this statement speak to you?

2. Witness to the gospel, and integrally to the claims of social justice, is not optional for those of us who bear the name Christian.

How do you feel called to witness to the gospel?

3. What else in this chapter was important to you?

Pray

In joy of spirit, let us acclaim Christ, who sits at the right hand of the Father:
Lord Jesus, you are the King of glory.

King of glory, you took with you our frail humanity to be glorified in heaven; remove the sins of the world,
—and restore us to the innocence which was ours before the Fall.
You came down from heaven on a pilgrimage of love,
—grant that we may take the same path to your presence.
You promised to draw all things to yourself,
—do not allow any one of us to be separated from your body.
Where you have gone before us in glory,
—may we follow you in mind and heart.
True God, we await your coming as our judge,

—may we see the vision of your glory and
your mercy in company with all the dead.
Let us pray
[that the risen Christ
will lead us to eternal life]
God our Father,
make us joyful
in the ascension of your Son Jesus Christ.
May we follow him into the new creation,
for his ascension is our glory and our hope.
We ask this through our Lord Jesus Christ,
    your Son
who lives and reigns with you and the Holy
    Spirit,
one God, for ever and ever. Amen.

—From the Liturgy of the Hours

SEVEN

He Will Come Again to Judge the Living and the Dead

Taken up to heaven and glorified forty days after his Resurrection, Christ has not left us alone. He dwells now on earth in and through his Church by virtue of the power of the Holy Spirit. We are not left orphans. The renewal of the world is irrevocably under way. The Church is endowed with a sanctity that is real, albeit imperfect. One does not have to look too far to understand this reality.

The supreme deception regarding religion or faith is the idea of a utopia without God here on earth, a world that is completely secular where there is no room for God. Admittedly, although his victory is definitive, things of this world are not yet fully subject to Christ. That is why we pray, especially in the Eucharist, to hasten Christ's return—"Marana tha" (1 Cor 16:22)—O Lord, come!

"According to the Lord, the present time is the time of the Spirit and of witness, but also a time still marked by 'distress' and the trial of evil which does not spare the Church (cf. Acts 1:8; 1 Cor 7:26; Eph 5:16; 1 Pet 4:17) and ushers in the struggles of the last days. It is a time of waiting and watching (cf. Mt 25:1, 13; Mk 13:33–37; 1 Jn 2:18; 4:3; 1 Tim 4:1)" (CCC 672). The Catechism continues: "Before Christ's second coming the Church must pass through a final trial that will shake the faith of many believers (cf. Lk 18:8; Mt 24:12)" (CCC 675). We need not fear, however. The Lord is still with us. "God's triumph over the revolt of evil will take the form of the Last Judgment after the final cosmic upheaval of this passing world" (CCC 677).

It is impossible to speak of the Last Judgment, when Christ will come in glory to judge the living and the dead and achieve the definitive triumph of good over evil, without conjuring up the magnificent fresco by Michelangelo on the wall of the Sistine Chapel. It is a powerful, terrifying Christ dominating the world as the dead rise to be rewarded or punished according to their deeds.

In the account given in Matthew 25:31–46, when the Son of Man comes in glory all the nations will be assembled before him. He separates the sheep from the goats—the sheep on his right and the goats on his left. He invites those on his right to inherit the kingdom prepared for them. "For I was hungry and you gave me food, I was thirsty and you gave me drink, a stranger and you welcomed me, naked and you clothed me, ill and you cared for me, in prison and you visited me." This sets a very practical standard: If you loved the least among you, you loved Jesus and have a claim on life everlasting.

In contrast, there are those on his left. To these people the Son of Man says: "Depart from me, you accursed, into the eternal fire prepared for the devil and his angels. For I was hungry and you gave me no food, I was thirsty and you gave me no drink, a stranger and you gave me no welcome, naked and you gave me no clothing, ill and in prison, and you did not care for me." For "Amen, I say to you, whatever you did for one of these least brothers of mine, you did for me."

"When he comes at the end of time to judge the living and the dead, the glorious Christ will reveal the secret disposition of hearts and will render to each man according to his works and according to his acceptance or refusal of grace" (CCC 682). Christ, after all, is truth and goodness personified. His second coming will unmask our greedy dishonesty and selfish malice. He will appear before the whole human race. Presently, he reveals himself to us in signs and sacraments. Then, he will confront all people directly and immediately. Our human solidarity will be revealed at the second coming. The day of individualism, tribalism, and nationalism will finally be over. Another dimension of the second coming, the radical and lasting importance of our human freedom, is highlighted. Whether for good or for evil, our free decisions have eternal consequences.

Although the second coming may not seem real or immediate or threatening to most of us, or even of overwhelming significance in our lives, we simply cannot ignore it. If we do, we do so at our own risk, closing our eyes to this article of our faith and the biblical evidence in support thereof—that Jesus will come in glory to judge the living and the dead.

In his book on the creed, O'Collins speaks of a relative of his who wanted to have "Amazing Grace" sung at her funeral. He writes that "her instinct is profoundly right." For "what will ultimately matter at the end will not be our good deeds or bad deeds, but the love of God shining through the compassionate face of Christ. His mercy, rather than our freedom, will have the final word." With added hope, then, we pray: "Come, Lord Jesus."

Reflect

1. "Amen, I say to you, whatever you did for one of these least brothers of mine, you did for me."

    Who are the least brothers of Jesus that you meet in your life?

2. Whether for good or for evil, our free decisions have eternal consequences.

    When has an action of yours had consequences you could not have expected?

3. What else in this chapter was important to you?

Pray

> Lord, make me an instrument of your peace.
> Where there is hatred, let me sow love;
> where there is injury, pardon;
> where there is doubt, faith;
> where there is despair, hope;
> where there is darkness, light;
> and where there is sadness, joy.
> O Divine Master, grant that I may not so
> much seek
> to be consoled as to console;
> to be understood as to understand;
> to be loved as to love.
> For it is in giving that we receive;
> it is in pardoning that we are pardoned;
> and it is in dying that we are born to eternal
> life. Amen.

—Saint Francis of Assisi

EIGHT

I Believe in the Holy Spirit

A fter the Father and the Son, the third divine person of the Blessed Trinity is the Holy Spirit. The Holy Spirit is perhaps the most mysterious of the three persons of the Trinity. Yet when we profess our faith each Sunday we do so precisely by the grace of the Holy Spirit.

Because he was the last to be revealed to us and because he was revealed in a gradual manner through the course of salvation history, the Holy Spirit is sometimes thought of as the "forgotten person" of the Trinity. But as the *United States Catholic Catechism for Adults* reminds us, "From the beginning, he is a part of the loving plan of our salvation from sin and of the offer of divine life" (*USCCA* 105).

The Catechism makes it very clear at the outset that "the Holy Spirit is at work with the Father and the Son from the beginning to the completion of the plan for our salvation" (*CCC* 686). The fourth-century Father of the Church Gregory of Nazianzus described the gradual revelation of the Holy Spirit as the "divine pedagogy" by which God teaches humanity his plan for our salvation throughout history.

Although the joint work of the Father and Spirit remains hidden and veiled until the "fullness of time," mention is made early on in the Old Testament of the Spirit. I think of Psalm 51, which we pray in the Liturgy of the Hours every Friday morning:

> A clean heart create for me, God;
> renew in me a steadfast spirit.
> Do not drive me from your presence,

nor take from me your holy spirit. (Ps 51:12–
13)

The Nicene Creed teaches us furthermore that the Spirit
"has spoken through the Prophets." The words of the prophet
Isaiah regarding the Spirit are the very ones Jesus chose to use
as he announced his mission at his inaugural address in the
synagogue at Nazareth (Lk 4:16–21):

> The Spirit of the Lord is upon me,
>> because he has anointed me
>>> to bring glad tidings to the poor.
> He has sent me to proclaim liberty to captives
>> and recovery of sight to the blind,
>>> to let the oppressed go free,
> and to proclaim a year acceptable to the Lord.

As the "fullness of time" drew near, John the Baptist was
"filled with the holy Spirit even from his mother's womb" (Lk
1:15). The presence of the Holy Spirit was even more explicitly revealed in the Blessed Mother. The Catechism teaches that
"in Mary, the Holy Spirit *fulfills* the plan of the Father's loving goodness. Through the Holy Spirit, the Virgin conceives
and gives birth to the Son of God. By the Holy Spirit's power
and her faith, her virginity became uniquely fruitful (Cf. Lk
1:26–38; Rom 4:18–21; Gal 4:26–28)" (*CCC* 723).

When at last Jesus came he did not reveal the Holy Spirit
fully or immediately, but only when he himself had been glorified through his death and resurrection. Nevertheless, Jesus
alluded to the Spirit little by little and gradually made him
known. For example, in speaking to Nicodemus (Jn 3:1–21)
Jesus said: "Amen, amen, I say to you, no one can enter the
kingdom of God without being born of water and Spirit. What
is born of flesh is flesh and what is born of spirit is spirit."
And to the Samaritan woman Jesus said: "But the hour is coming, and is now here, when true worshipers will worship the
Father in Spirit and truth; and indeed the Father seeks such

people to worship him. God is Spirit, and those who worship him must worship in Spirit and truth" (Jn 4:4–30). From our perspective, after the resurrection, we can see that ". . . Christ's whole work is in fact a joint mission of the Son and the Holy Spirit" (*CCC* 727).

The Spirit is fully revealed on Pentecost. The key locus is the upper room, the same room in which Jesus had gathered with his disciples on Holy Thursday, the night before he died and instituted the Eucharist and the priesthood. It was also the place where Saint John locates the longest farewell address in history—Jesus' leave-taking of his disciples. This farewell discourse occupies five chapters (Jn 13–17) of Saint John's Gospel.

In *The Sacrament of Charity*, Benedict XVI refers to the "farewell discourse" in John, stating: "Jesus clearly relates [there] the gift of his life in the paschal mystery to the gift of the Spirit to his own (cf. Jn 16:7). Once risen, bearing in his flesh the signs of the passion, he can pour out the Spirit upon them (cf. Jn 20:22), making them sharers in his own mission (cf. Jn 20:21)" (*SC* 12).

It is precisely there in the upper room on the night before he died that Jesus promised and predicted that he would send the Holy Spirit. We need not wait liturgically until Pentecost to speak of the Holy Spirit. Jesus spoke of the Holy Spirit the very night before he died. In fact, the Holy Spirit comes as the price of Christ's departure. "But I tell you the truth, it is better for you that I go. For if I do not go, the Advocate will not come to you. But if I go, I will send him to you" (Jn 16:7). Christ will send "another Advocate" (Jn 14:16), the Spirit of truth, the Paraclete,"a term that describes him as advocate and consoler" (*USCCA* 103). "The Advocate, the holy Spirit that the Father will send in my name—he will teach you everything and remind you of all that [I] told you" (Jn 14:26).

He "will teach . . . and bring . . . to . . . remembrance." Not only does that mean that the Holy Spirit will continue to inspire the spreading of the gospel in our time, but it also means that the Spirit will help us understand the correct meaning of Christ's message and that we will be inspired by the power of the Holy Spirit.

In the upper room on the night before he died, Jesus was preparing his disciples, and us today, for the challenge of continuing his mission. The Holy Spirit was essential for this. In a special way, the disciples were to be associated with the Holy Spirit. "When the Advocate comes whom I will send you from the Father, the Spirit of truth that proceeds from the Father, he will testify to me. And you also testify, because you have been with me from the beginning" (Jn 15:26–27). The Spirit would teach us: "I have much more to tell you, but you cannot bear it now. But when he comes, the Spirit of truth, he will guide you to all truth" (Jn 16:12–13). Jesus is describing the Holy Spirit to them. The Spirit will help them to remember what Jesus taught them: The Spirit will guide them into all the truth, the Spirit will bear witness to him, and in turn they will bear witness to him also.

After his resurrection from the dead, Jesus returned to the upper room, in the words of John 20:19, "on the evening of that first day of the week," i.e., on Easter Sunday night. It is the Johannine Pentecost. It is there that he twice gave them his peace and breathed on them and said to them: "Receive the holy Spirit. Whose sins you forgive are forgiven them, and whose sins you retain are retained" (Jn 20:22–23).

As explained by our late Holy Father John Paul II in his third encyclical letter, *Dominum et Vivificantem* (*The Lord and Giver of Life*), promulgated on Pentecost 1986:

> [Jesus] fulfilled the principal prediction of the farewell discourse: the Risen Christ, as it were beginning a new creation, *"brings" to the apostles the Holy Spirit*. He brings him at the price of his own "departure": he gives them this Spirit as it were through the wounds of his crucifixion: "He showed them

> his hands and his side." It is in the power of this
> crucifixion that he says to them: "Receive the Holy
> Spirit." (*DEV* 24)

Yes, in that same upper room, the promise of the Holy Spirit was made, and the sending of the Holy Spirit to the disciples gathered there took place!

When we think of the Holy Spirit, most of us probably think of Luke's account of the first Pentecost in the Acts of the Apostles 2:1–13. Fifty days after Easter, the disciples were all huddled together in fear behind locked doors. Then suddenly a wind roared through the house filling every room. People from every known country of the world were gathered in Jerusalem for the Jewish harvest feast. They heard this roaring wind. Then tongues of fire, representing the Holy Spirit, came down upon the apostles. It filled them with the Holy Spirit and made it possible for them to be understood in every language. Immediately the apostles went out and began to preach the crucified and risen Jesus. Filled with boldness and courage because of the Holy Spirit, they proclaimed the mighty works of God. Three thousand people were added to their number that day. This is what can happen when we really yield to the power of the Holy Spirit. It can and does happen in our lives.

The Holy Spirit has been with the Church ever since, making us alive: "The Holy Spirit is dynamic, transforming our bodies into temples of God and our souls into dwelling places for Christ. . . . The Holy Spirit wants to fill us with inspiration and encouragement"(*USCCA* 103).

In that great document of the Vatican Council, the *Dogmatic Constitution on Divine Revelation* (*Dei Verbum*), we learn: "The Tradition that comes from the Apostles makes progress in the Church, with the help of the Holy Spirit" (*DV* 8). The Spirit is life giving. The Spirit is an experience of God's love.

Both the *Catechism of the Catholic Church* and the *United States Catholic Catechism for Adults* set forth eight ways by

which we come to know the Holy Spirit and experience him
in the life of the Church:

> in the Scriptures he inspired;
> in the Tradition, to which the Church Fathers
> are always timely witnesses;
> in the Church Magisterium, which [the Spirit]
> assists;
> in the sacramental liturgy, through its words
> and symbols, in which the Holy Spirit puts us
> into communion with Christ;
> in prayer, wherein he intercedes for us;
> in the charisms and ministries by which the
> Church is built up;
> in the signs of apostolic and missionary life;
> in the witness of saints through whom [the
> Spirit] manifests his holiness and continues the
> work of salvation. (*CCC* 688, cf. *USCCA* 106)

In the fifth century, a monk known as Mark the Hermit
used to ask: How do I know I have the Holy Spirit within
me? In the same way, he answered, as a mother knows she
is pregnant. There is life within her. The life within us is the
Holy Spirit.

A parent may be having a difficult time dealing with a
teenager, to use a simple example, and may not be sure of
what to do. The parent is almost out of energy in dealing with
the challenges presented. He or she prays to the Holy Spirit
for enthusiasm. And the gifts and fruits of the Holy Spirit will
blossom in that person—patience, courage, wisdom, counsel.

There is a dynamism that takes hold of us when we pray
to the Holy Spirit. The disciples received the gifts of the Holy
Spirit at Pentecost in the upper room, and they became dynamic missionaries and were thereafter willing to suffer for
Christ with their lives. So is that possible with us too, if only
we learn to beg and pray to the Holy Spirit for his gifts. The

Holy Spirit is the breath of prayer. The Holy Spirit is also the gift who comes into our hearts.

It is the same Holy Spirit who comes to us in Baptism. In that sacrament we become temples of the Holy Spirit and our sins are washed away. We were made children of God the Father and members of the Body of Christ.

At Confirmation, the bishop seals us with chrism and the Holy Spirit is conferred upon us to enable us to be strengthened to pursue the mission of Christ to transform the world. In his apostolic letter on the Eucharist, Pope Benedict said wisely: "It is through the working of the Spirit that Christ himself continues to be present and active in his Church, starting with her vital center which is the Eucharist" (*SC* 12). He states further that "against this backdrop we can understand the decisive role played by the Holy Spirit in the eucharistic celebration, particularly with regard to transubstantiation" (*SC* 13).

After recognizing how "all life" and "all holiness" come by the working of the Holy Spirit, the third Eucharistic Prayer at Mass invokes God's Spirit:

And so Father, we bring you these gifts,
we ask you to make them holy
by the power of your Spirit,
that they may become the Body and Blood of your Son,
our Lord Jesus Christ,
at whose command we celebrate this Eucharist.

In the second Eucharistic Prayer we hear the priest's prayer to the Father:

Let your Spirit come upon these gifts to make them holy
so that they may become for us the Body and Blood
of our Lord, Jesus Christ.

And so in the power of the Holy Spirit, bread and wine are transformed into his Body and Blood by the ministry of the priest.

When it comes to the Holy Spirit, the first thing the Catechism does is to cite Saint Paul: "No one can say, 'Jesus is Lord,' except by the holy Spirit" (1 Cor 12:3). To be in touch with Christ and his life, we must first have been touched by the Holy Spirit. You and I, initiated into the Catholic life by Baptism, Confirmation, and the Eucharist, must daily implore the life-giving assistance of the Holy Spirit. The gifts of the Holy Spirit must be received and accepted. If we yield to these gifts and use them, we will readily see their fruits in our daily lives—charity, joy, peace, patience, kindness, goodness, generosity, gentleness, faithfulness, modesty, self-control, and chastity (cf. Gal 5:22–23).

The term *spirit* translates the Hebrew word *ruah*, which in its first sense means "breath," "air," or "wind." Think of the images used to describe the Holy Spirit. The Catechism lists nine of them: water (Holy Spirit's action at Baptism); anointing (with oil at Confirmation); fire (transforming energy symbolized in the tongues of fire); cloud and light (appearances of God in the Old Testament and New Testament); seal (indelible effect of the anointing); hand (healing through laying-on of his hand); finger (finger to cast out demons); and the dove (over Christ at his baptism) (cf. CCC 694–701).

Finally, the Holy Spirit is God's gift of love to us and to his Church. It is the Spirit who is the source of new life in Christ. The mission of Christ and the Holy Spirit is brought to completion in the Church, which is the body of Christ and the temple of the Holy Spirit. "The Holy Spirit, whom Christ the head [of the Church] pours out on his members, builds, animates, and sanctifies the Church" (CCC 747). In the words of Saint Cyril of Alexandria: "For just as the power of Christ's sacred flesh unites those in whom it dwells into one body, I think that in the same way the one and undivided Spirit of God, who dwells in all, leads all into spiritual unity [Footnote: St. Cyril of Alexandria, *In Jo. ev.*, 11, 11: PG 74, 561]" (CCC 738). Come Holy Spirit!

Reflect

1. In the fifth century, a monk known as Mark the
    Hermit used to ask: How do I know I have the Holy
    Spirit within me?

    How would you answer that question for yourself?

2. Think of the nine images used to describe the Holy
    Spirit: water, anointing with oil, fire, cloud, light,
    seal, hand, finger, and dove.

    Which of these images best fits with your experi-
    ence of the Holy Spirit?

3. What else in this chapter was important to you?

Pray

Come Holy Spirit, fill the hearts of your faithful
and kindle in them the fire of your love.
Send forth your Spirit and they shall be created.
And You shall renew the face of the earth.

O, God, who by the light of the Holy Spirit, did instruct
the hearts of the faithful, grant that by the same Holy
Spirit we may be truly wise and ever enjoy his consolations, Through Christ Our Lord, Amen.

NINE

The Holy Catholic Church, the Communion of Saints

Ilove the Catholic Church and everything about it—from the incense, the May crowning, and the Corpus Christi procession, to the coffee and doughnuts, the friendship with similarly minded people, and the many forms of social outreach to those in need. And these are just a few of the things I love.

My love affair began with my Baptism when I was incorporated into a living and diverse community at Sacred Heart Church on Sixteenth Street in Washington, D.C. It has been the most important affiliation and commitment of my life. Being a member of the Catholic Church continues daily to change and transform my very being and the way I view the world. It is the Church where I also receive the Eucharist every day, where I regularly receive the healing sacrament of Penance, where I received the fullness of the Holy Spirit at Confirmation, where I was privileged to be ordained a priest in the sacrament of Holy Orders at the Cathedral of Saint Matthew the Apostle in Washington. And it is the Church where I hope to receive the Anointing of the Sick when my time comes and so be prepared to meet the Lord Jesus forever in heaven, the new and eternal Jerusalem.

While the Church nurtures our faith, it is also the object of our faith. In the ninth article of the Apostles' Creed we profess: "I believe . . . in the holy catholic Church" or as we say each Sunday in the Nicene Creed: "We believe in one holy catholic and apostolic Church."

Why do we love the Church? Why should we love the Church? What is the basis of our belief in the Church? Despite its human wounds, foibles, and disappointments, the Church is also divine. It is Christ's Church, after all. It is his living body. He shines out visibly from the Church. It is Jesus, in the power of his Holy Spirit, who continues to entice and draw each one of us to his Church. We are his people. How else could this institution, this world wide community, have remained so faithful and continued throughout the last two thousand years if it were merely a human institution? No human explanation can begin to account for the longevity of the Church. Think of the empires, countries, and corporations that have arisen and disappeared from the face of the earth in a much shorter time. I am reminded of a text from the Acts of the Apostles where, speaking of the work of the apostles, the lawyer Gamaliel said: "For if this endeavor or this activity is of human origin, it will destroy itself. But if it comes from God, you will not be able to destroy them; you may even find yourselves fighting against God" (Acts 5:38–39). The Church is of God.

The Catechism expresses this aptly: "The Church is both visible and spiritual, a hierarchical society and the Mystical Body of Christ. She is one, yet formed of two components, human and divine. That is her mystery, which only faith can accept" (CCC 779).

We name this "mystery" the Church. The English word *church* is a translation of the Hebrew word *qahal*, the Greek *ekklesia*, and the Latin *ecclesia* (all meaning "gathering of people" or "community"). The Church is trinitarian in nature and has been progressively revealed by God in history and prepared for over the centuries.

The Church was born in the Father's heart, foreshadowed in the designs of creation, and prepared for by the election of the Hebrew people as God's Chosen People. It was the Father's plan for sharing divine life with all people. "In the fullness of time," the Church was finally instituted by Christ as he hung dying on the Cross and symbolized by the blood and water that flowed from the pierced side of Christ. And the Holy Spirit was sent, as the permanent gift of Easter, to sanctify the Church continually, to give us life. This life we share is the life of the risen Lord, his Spirit. "So forceful is the presence of the Spirit in the life of the early Church that the New Testament narrative of the Church's early growth, the Acts of the Apostles, is often called the 'Gospel of the Holy Spirit'" (*USCCA* 114).

The Church will receive its perfection only in the glory of heaven. Until that day, the Church, in the words of Saint Augustine, "progresses on her pilgrimage amidst this world's persecutions and God's consolations." And there is not a one of us who has not experienced some form of persecution even in our day for being Catholic. Hopefully, each one of us has had our share of consolations as well.

What is most important to remember is that the Church exists fundamentally for our holiness here and now and for our salvation in eternity. The primary purpose of the Church is to make us holy, to bring us each day into communion with God, especially through the sacraments, which are instruments of holiness, the very instruments of our salvation.

In *The Sacrament of Charity*, Benedict XVI underscores the relationship between the Eucharist and the Church. The Church was born when water and blood flowed from the pierced side of Christ, with water representing Baptism and blood the Eucharist.

> Since the Eucharist makes present Christ's redeeming sacrifice, we must start by acknowledging that "there is a causal influence of the Eucharist at the Church's very origins." The Eucharist is Christ who gives himself to us and continually builds us up as his body. Hence, there is a striking interplay between the Eucharist which builds up the Church,

and the Church herself which "makes" the Eucharist. . . . The Church's ability to "make" the Eucharist
is completely rooted in Christ's self-gift to her. (*SC*
14)

The Catechism sets forth three very rich images to help us
capture and begin to understand the inexhaustible mystery
that is the Church. No one image can suffice. First, the Church
is the People of God (which was the paramount image of the
Church from the Second Vatican Council). Second, the Church
is the Body of Christ. And finally, the Church is the Temple of
the Holy Spirit. Let us examine for now just this first image.

The People of God—the Church

We become members of the People of God, the Church,
by Baptism and faith. Like the Israelites of old, we too are
chosen as members of God's holy people. This image links
us with our Jewish roots, this sense of being a chosen people.
There are certain characteristics of the Church as the People
of God.

- God is not the property of any people, but rather the
  Church belongs to God. He acquired it as a people
  of his own, "a chosen race, a royal priesthood, a holy
  nation" (1 Pt 2:9).

- One does not becomes a member by physical birth,
  but by faith and Baptism.

- Jesus Christ is the head of the Church.

- The Holy Spirit dwells in the hearts of this people as
  in a temple.

- The law of the Church is the new commandment of
  love, the new "law" of the Holy Spirit.

- The Church's mission is to be salt of the earth and

light of the world.

- Its destiny is the Kingdom of God that has already begun and will be brought to perfection by him at the end of time (cf. *CCC* 782).

Three Offices of Christ

Now what kind of people are we by virtue of our Baptism? We share in three "offices" or functions of Christ, in the very mission of Jesus in our day. As laity and clergy, we share, although in different ways, in the mission of Jesus as priest, prophet, and king. We are priestly, prophetic, and kingly people. There are a dignity and an equality in the eyes of God that each of us, laity and clergy, shares precisely because of our Baptism.

Baptized members of the laity share in the priesthood of Jesus Christ. It is referred to as the "common priesthood of all the faithful" (*USCCA* 117). The spiritual sacrifice offered at Mass is uniquely at the heart of the ordained or ministerial priesthood. "The ministerial priesthood differs in essence from the common priesthood of the faithful because it confers a sacred power for the service of the faithful" (*CCC* 1592).

The laity share, first, in the priestly mission of Jesus when they offer spiritual sacrifices each day to the Father by their works, prayers, apostolic endeavors, family and married life, daily work, relaxation of mind and body; "if they are accomplished in the Spirit—indeed even the hardships of life if patiently born—all these become spiritual sacrifices (*LG* 34; cf. *LG* 10; 1 Pet 2:5)" and a share in the mission of Christ as priest (*CCC* 901).

Second, the laity likewise share in the prophetic mission of Jesus by concrete works of evangelization. This means teaching and witnessing God's holy Word in our secular world. "Saint Francis of Assisi once said, 'Preach always. Sometimes use words'" (*USCCA* 117). This is possible first when a lay person falls in love with God's holy Word—a Word that transforms us and makes it possible for us to see the world through Christian eyes and ultimately to act in the ways of Jesus.

And finally the laity share in the kingly mission of Jesus every time they engage the secular world in the direction of loving service for peace, justice, and joy. Christ the King is a servant king, a lamb led to the slaughter. When we serve, especially the least among us, we share in the mission today of Jesus as king.

Four Characteristics of the Church

At the heart of this section of the Catechism on the Church is the teaching on the four characteristics or marks of the Church. They are inseparably linked among themselves and indicate essential features of the Church and her mission. Following the ancient Nicene Creed, we believe that the Church is one, holy, catholic, and apostolic. "Because of the sinfulness of the Church's members, these marks are not always lived out fully, so we need to view them as both a reality and yet a challenge" (*USCCA* 127).

These four characteristics are not simply adjectives that describe the Church. They are gifts of God that mark the Church and, more importantly, they describe tasks and duties for each generation of believers to assume. What the Church is defines what the Church is supposed to do. The Church's very nature is realized in its mission.

The Church is one. "There is neither Jew nor Greek, there is neither slave nor free person, there is not male and female; for you are all one in Christ Jesus" (Gal 3:28). Unity is at the essence of the Church. It reflects the unity of the Trinity. The Church comes from one source—God the Father; was founded by one Lord Jesus Christ; and lives by one soul, the Holy Spirit—the same Spirit "who brings about that wonderful

communion of the faithful and joins them together so inti-
mately in Christ that he is the principle of the church's unity
(*UR* 2 para. 2)" (*CCC* 813).

What are the bonds of unity? Above all, they are charity, a
common faith, common worship (especially the sacraments),
and a common life under the successors of the apostles. Unity
does not mean uniformity. From the beginning, the Church
has been marked by a genuine diversity. One need only be in
Saint Peter's Square at Rome on any Sunday to witness the
variety of cultures or at any downtown parish in a large city.
But there is a unity of the essentials.

The Second Vatican Council taught that the Church of
Christ "subsists" (continues to exist) fully in the Catholic
Church. It is only in the Catholic Church that the "fullness of
the means of salvation can be obtained" although many of the
elements of holiness and truth that constitute the Church and
give her life exist outside her visible boundaries (*CCC* 816,
819). Christ gives the Church the gift of unity.

Tragically, throughout the centuries divisions have de-
veloped among Christians. But where there is division, the
Church must pray and work to maintain, reinforce, and perfect the unity that Christ wills for her. This was Jesus' will,
expressed in his prayer at the Last Supper: "that they may all
be one, as you, Father, are in me and I in you, that they also
may be in us, that the world may believe that you sent me"
(Jn 17:21). The Catholic Church has always been committed,
through the ecumenical movement, to the restoration of unity
among Christians.

> Ecumenism includes efforts to pray together, joint
> study of the Scripture and of one another's tradi-
> tions, common action for social justice, and dia-
> logue in which the leaders and theologians of the
> different churches and communities discuss in
> depth their doctrinal and theological positions for

greater mutual understanding, and "to work for
unity in truth (*UUS*, nos. 18, 29)." (*USCCA* 128)

The Church is holy. "The Church . . . is held, as a matter of
faith, to be unfailingly holy." Why? Because "Christ, the Son
of God, who with the Father and the Spirit is hailed as 'alone
holy,' loved the Church as his Bride, giving himself up for her
so as to sanctify her (*LG* 39; cf. Eph 5:25–26)" (i.e., to make her
holy) (*CCC* 823). He died to make us holy. Since the origin of
the Church is in the Trinity, that divine life is also the source of
her holiness. Holiness, which means to be set apart, belongs
fully to God alone. But in Baptism, each of us no longer stands
"outside," but each of us comes to share in the very holiness
of God—albeit imperfectly realized in the life of the Church.
Each of us is called to be holy, yet there exists that continual
struggle with the forces of evil. We need not look beyond the
tips of our noses to understand this. The Church is, however,
essentially holy and a consecrated community, but also a community in constant need of reform and renewal.

"By *canonizing* some of the faithful, i.e., by solemnly proclaiming that they practiced heroic virtue and lived in fidelity
to God's grace, the Church recognizes the power of the Spirit
of holiness within her and sustains the hope of believers by
proposing the saints to them as models and intercessors (cf.
LG 40; 48–51)" (*CCC* 828). The Church continues to add new
witnesses to the list of saints in the Americas and around the
world.

As Catholics, we believe in the "communion of saints."
That includes all the faithful of Christ, those who are still pilgrims on earth (you and me, for example), the dead who are
being purified in purgatory, and the blessed in heaven. All
together, they—and we—form one Church, one communion
of saints. It is this communion that helps make the Church
holy—the power, the miracle of prayer—each of us praying
for one another.

The Church is catholic. The word *catholic* means "univer-sal" in the sense of "having the character of totality or whole-ness." The Catechism gives two reasons why the Church is catholic. First, the Church is catholic because Christ is present in her (*CCC* 830). Second, she is catholic because Christ has given her the mission to the whole human race. God wills the salvation of everyone. By her very nature, the Church is a universal missionary body. The Church exists to evangelize. It is a requirement of the Church's catholicity (*CCC* 831). She proclaims the fullness of the faith. The Church exists in every country of the world, visibly there—even in minority status or under persecution in some countries.

No one is excluded from the call to evangelize. Each of us in the Church has our own area of mission. That is our con-tinual challenge. That is the continual challenge to be catholic. There is room in the Church for a variety of charisms: the la-ity, priests, deacons, bishops, and the pope, men and women of religious orders, secular institutes, societies of apostolic life, hermits, virgins. Each one has his or her own unique gift to offer. What a beautiful tapestry of Christian life coming to-gether as one and reaching out to all!

Who belongs to the Catholic Church? The Catechism is clear:

> Fully incorporated into the society of the Church are those who, possessing the Spirit of Christ, ac-cept all the means of salvation given to the Church together with her entire organization, and who—by the bonds constituted by the profession of faith, the sacraments, ecclesiastical government, and communion—are joined in the visible structure of the Church of Christ, who rules through the Su-preme Pontiff and the bishops (*LG* 14). (*CCC* 837)

In contrast, those who "'do not profess the Catholic faith in its entirety or have not preserved unity or communion under the successor of Peter' (*LG* 15) . . . [but] 'who believe in Christ and have been properly baptized are put in a certain, although imperfect, communion with the Catholic Church' (*UR* 3)" (*CCC* 838). The catechism speaks also of Jews, Muslims, and those of other non-Christian religions and explains how each is related to the People of God in various ways (*CCC* 839–843).

The Church is apostolic. She is built on a lasting foundation: "the twelve apostles of the Lamb" (Rev 21:14). She was founded on the apostles—the witnesses chosen and sent on mission by Christ himself. With the help of the Holy Spirit dwelling within her, the Church keeps and hands on the teaching, the "deposit of faith" received and handed down from the apostles.

In addition, the Church is preserved formally and officially by the bishops—successors of the apostles—in an unbroken chain from Peter until our day. They continue to teach, sanctify, and govern the Church, "assisted by priests, in union with the successor of Peter, the Church's supreme pastor (*AG* 5)" (*CCC* 857).

Christ governs the Church through Peter and the other apostles, who are present in their successors, the Pope and the college of bishops. "This pastoral office of Peter and the other apostles belongs to the Church's very foundation and is continued by the bishops under the primacy of the Pope" (*CCC* 881). The bishop of Rome, the Pope, enjoys by divine institution "full, supreme, and universal power over the whole Church, a power which he can always exercise unhindered (*LG* 22; cf. *CD* 2, 9)" (*CCC* 882). The individual bishop is the visible source and foundation of unity in his own particular church or diocese. "Helped by the priests, their co-workers, and by the deacons, the bishops have the duty of authentically teaching the faith, celebrating divine worship, above all the Eucharist, and guiding their Churches as true pastors. Their responsibility also includes concern for all the Churches, with and under the Pope" (*CCC* 939).

To preserve God's people from deviations and defections and to guarantee them the objective possibility of professing the true faith without error, "Christ endowed the Church's shepherds with the charism of infallibility in matters of faith and morals." (*CCC* 890). The Catechism explains clearly how this exercise takes place (*CCC* 891–92). The doctrine of infallibility is often misunderstood. The Pope can err when it comes to predicting the weather or the stock market. But under certain precise and limited conditions he cannot err: when he is speaking authoritatively as Pope, as the successor of Peter; when he is speaking to the entire Church; and when he is explicitly defining a doctrine of faith or morals. When these circumstances are in place, the Pope cannot err. The infallibility promised to the Church is also present in the body of bishops when, together with Peter's successor, they exercise their supreme teaching authority, above all in an ecumenical council. Such pronouncements "'must be adhered to with the obedience of faith. (*LG* 25 para. 2)' This infallibility extends as far as the deposit of divine Revelation itself (cf. *LG* 25)" (*CCC* 891).

With regard to non-infallible teachings of the ordinary magisterium that lead to "better understanding of Revelation in matters of faith and morals," the Church teaches that "the faithful 'are to adhere to it with religious assent (*LG* 25)' which, though distinct from the assent of faith, is nonetheless an extension of it" (*CCC* 892).

The Communion of Saints

One of the most consoling doctrines of our faith is that of the "communion of saints." It is a "communion of all the faithful of Christ, those who are pilgrims on earth, the dead who are being purified, and the blessed in heaven, all together forming one Church [Footnote: Paul VI, *CPG* para. 30]" (*CCC*

962). They form, as it were, different stages in belonging to the Church. Normally we focus on this beautiful teaching at the beginning of November as we celebrate All Saints Day and All Souls Day. In a special fashion, on those days each year, we remember those "holy men and women of every time and place" (Preface, All Saints) and we pray for "all our departed brothers and sisters" (Preface, All Souls) that they might forever share in the risen life of our Lord and Savior.

This ancient doctrine of the communion of saints is best expressed by Paul VI, who wrote that "each individual son of God in Christ and through Christ is joined by a wonderful link to the life of all his other Christian brothers [and sisters] in the supernatural unity of the Mystical Body of Christ till, as it were, a single mystical person is formed" (ID 5).

We know instinctively, and we believe, that those in heaven are praying for us. In the back of my parish in Bethesda, Maryland, a church named after Saint Thérèse of Lisieux, the Little Flower, there is a saying of hers that is etched on the wall surrounding her beautiful marble statue: "I want to spend my heaven in doing good on earth." I have great confidence that, like all the saints, she is interceding in prayer for me and those who seek her intercession. It is her special vocation and the vocation of all those gone before us who live with the Lord Jesus and all the angels and saints.

As each of us is called to pray for the dead, we know that, in that same way, those with the Lord, and those in purgatory, are praying for us. What a great sense of consolation we can find in the one Church, a "communion of prayer," each praying for the other, from the exalted heavenly choir to those being purified in purgatory to the rest of us here on earth advancing daily on our way to the heavenly Jerusalem.

All together, we form one Church, one communion of saints. It is this communion that helps make the Church holy—the power and miracle of prayer—each of us praying for one another. I think of the memorial cards that fill my breviary:

some of classmates, ordained priests, and others of loved ones already gone to the Lord. What a sense of communion! There is no article in the Creed that resonates more with the experience and practice of faithful Christians who find deep links in the communion of saints and evidence of holiness in the Church. In the power of prayer within this communion of saints, no Christian is ever left alone or defenseless. Could there be any greater sense of consolation and confidence in the Lord Jesus and those who seek his help in the body of Christ? This article of the Creed is not merely based on theology; its fruits are experienced in prayer.

The Church and Her Mother, Mary

In *The Sacrament of Charity*, Benedict XVI reminds us that Mary "was given by . . . Christ Jesus, dying on the Cross, as a mother to his disciple, with these words: 'Woman, behold your Son'" (Jn 19:27, *SC* 33). From the Cross, Mary thus becomes the Mother of the Church. "In her we find realized most perfectly the essence of the Church" (*SC* 96).

The *United States Catholic Catechism for Adults* says of Mary—Mother of Christ, Mother of the Church—"She is the first and greatest of all the disciples of Christ" (*USCCA* 143). The Catechism further comments on her faithfulness: "By her complete adherence to the Father's will, to his Son's redemptive work, and to every prompting of the Holy Spirit, the Virgin Mary is the Church's model of faith and charity. Thus she is a 'preeminent and . . . wholly unique member of the Church'; indeed, she is the 'exemplary realization' (*LG* 53; 63) . . . of the Church" (*CCC* 967). And it explains her role in relation to the Church and to all humanity: "In a wholly singular way she cooperated by her obedience, faith, hope, and burning charity in the Savior's work of restoring supernatural life to souls. For this reason she is a mother to us in the order of grace (*LG* 61)" (*CCC* 968).

At the beginning of the third session of the Second Vatican Council, Paul VI announced that Mary would be honored under the title Mother of the Church. "Like Mary, the Church has a maternal role, giving birth to people in Christ. The Church can never cease to look at Mary, who gave birth to Jesus Christ" (*USCCA* 146). We need only think of the Easter Vigil around the world and the number of new Catholics who are reborn that night in Baptism or who are embraced into full communion with the Church.

One important point: Catholics do not worship Mary or place her on equal footing with her Son! At the same time, from the beginning of the Church, Christians have sought Mary's prayers and assistance. She is a powerful intercessor. Remember her words and actions at the wedding feast at Cana: "Do whatever he tells you," she said to the servants (Jn 2:5). Mary always leads us to her Son.

We can draw consolation and certain hope from Mary because we believe that Mary, the Mother of Christ and Mother of the Church, continues in heaven to exercise her maternal and intercessory role on our behalf. And together, we pray: Mary, Mother of the Church, pray for us.

Reflect

1. "I love the Catholic Church and everything about it. . . ."

   What do you love about being Catholic?

2. Three very rich images to help us capture and begin to understand the inexhaustible mystery that is the Church: the People of God, the Body of Christ, and the Temple of the Holy Spirit.

Which of these images do you find most strengthens your faith in the Church?

3. Saint Thérèse of Lisieux once said: "I want to spend my heaven in doing good on earth."

   Who do you believe is spending his or her heaven helping you here on earth?

4. What else in this chapter was important to you?

Pray

Father we thank Thee who has planted
Thy holy name within our hearts.
Knowledge and faith and life immortal
Jesus Thy Son to us imparts.
Thou, Lord, didst make all for Thy pleasure,
Didst give man food for all his days,
Giving in Christ the bread eternal;
Thine is the power, be Thine the praise.
Watch o'er Thy Church, O Lord, in mercy,
Save it from evil, guard it still,
Perfect it in Thy love, unite it,
Cleansed and conformed unto Thy will.
As grain, once scattered on the hillsides,
Was in the broken bread made one,
So from all lands Thy Church be gathered
Into Thy kingdom by Thy Son.

—From the Didache (AD 40–60)

TEN

The Forgiveness of Sins

When Jesus appeared to his apostles in the upper room on Easter evening he breathed upon them and gave them the gift of the Holy Spirit. "Peace be with you. . . . Receive the holy Spirit. Whose sins you forgive are forgiven them," he told them (Jn 20:19, 22–23).

In his farewell discourse Jesus had promised to send the Holy Spirit to his disciples: "When he comes," Jesus told them, "he will convict the world in regard to sin and righteousness and condemnation . . ." (Jn 16:8). With the word he, Jesus refers to the Holy Spirit, who "convicts" us of the reality of our sins. God sent the Holy Spirit among us for the forgiveness of our sins in the sacrament of Penance. Nor should we forget that the sacrament also has healing power. The origin of this sacrament is conveyed through the prayer of the priest in confession:

> God the Father of mercies,
> through the death and resurrection of his Son
> has reconciled the world to himself
> and sent the Holy Spirit among us
> for the forgiveness of sins. . . .

This prayer of absolution typifies the way Roman Catholics and other Christians acknowledge God's Spirit to be at work today, bringing life, holiness, and growth to a wounded human race. It is precisely by the power of the Holy Spirit that our sins are forgiven in sacramental confession. Each of us experiences in the words of absolution a newness of life.

I am reminded each year, especially around Christmas and Easter, when large numbers of people come to confession at the parish, that the sacrament is such an incredible experience of healing and of the liberating power of the Holy Spirit. Penitents experience firsthand the forgiveness of their sins and the transformation of their own concrete lives through the healing sacrament of Penance. Through the grace of this wonderful sacrament, our lives change, each one of ours, sometimes even radically.

This experience of the Holy Spirit would not have been possible if Jesus had not left that upper room and moved the next day to Calvary, to death on the Cross out of love for us. Christ's departure from the disciples, his death and resurrection, was an indispensable condition for the coming of the Holy Spirit. "If I do not go, the Advocate will not come to you. But if I go, I will send him to you" (Jn 16:7). His departure is thus linked to the very mystery of our redemption. The new life promised in the Holy Spirit can happen only as a result of Christ's self-emptying and death on the Cross.

Do we really believe, at the level of faith, that our sins can be forgiven, wiped away completely? Do we even acknowledge that we sin, that there is such a thing as sin? Do we believe that it is necessary that our sins be forgiven, and if so, why? Do we acknowledge that Jesus Christ suffered and died precisely that our sins might be forgiven? Do we believe that the risen Lord Jesus, on Easter Sunday night in the upper room, breathed on his disciples and said to them, "Receive the holy Spirit"? Do we believe that, after the resurrection, the risen Lord sent his disciples on mission so that "repentance, for the forgiveness of sins, would be preached in his name to all the nations" (Lk 24:47)?

Do we believe that Baptism is the first and chief sacrament of forgiveness of sins? Do we believe that it was Christ's will that the Church possess the power to forgive the sins of the baptized and that the Church exercises this power through her bishops and priests in the sacrament of Penance? Finally, do we truly understand and believe that the "sacrament of Penance is necessary for salvation for those who have fallen after Baptism, just as Baptism is necessary for salvation for those who have not yet been reborn [Footnote: Council of Trent (1551): *DS* 1672; cf. St. Gregory of Nazianzus, *Oratio* 39, 17: *PG* 36, 356]" (*CCC* 980)?

This is our faith! This is our precious Catholic faith! It is what is meant when we profess each Sunday: "I believe . . . in the forgiveness of sins." What a great gift that our God, who is rich in mercy, has given us through the Church!

The Catechism makes it clear that "there is no offense, however serious, that the Church cannot forgive" (*CCC* 982). As powerful as the grace of Baptism is, however, it does not deliver us from the weakness of human nature. If we are honest, we will admit that each of us must fight daily against the inclination toward evil.

There should be no joy greater than receiving the forgiveness of our sins in the sacrament of Penance. There should be no embarrassment in confessing our sins—and confessing them monthly or more often if necessary—for so integral is repentance to the Christian life and to our faith. The forgiveness of sins is a grace. Jesus' nail marks are signs of our salvation from sin. No source of joy could be greater than knowing that Jesus continues to forgive us today. What a supreme act of love from Jesus for us. "I tell you, in just the same way there will be more joy in heaven over one sinner who repents than over ninety-nine righteous people who have no need of repentance" (Lk 15:7). Please, do not deny him that opportunity.

Reflect

1. Why do you think it is so hard today for most people to admit that they have sinned?

2. Have you had an experience of healing and forgiveness in the sacrament of Penance that you can share?

3. What else in this chapter was important to you?

Pray

My God,
I am sorry for my sins with all my heart.
In choosing to do wrong and failing to do good,
I have sinned against you
whom I should love above all things.
I firmly intend, with your help,
to do penance, to sin no more,
and to avoid whatever leads me to sin.
Our Savior Jesus Christ suffered and died for us.
In his Name, my God, have mercy.

—From the Rite of Penance

ELEVEN

The Resurrection of the Body

The last two articles of the Apostles' Creed treat what
are traditionally called the "the four last things": death,
judgment, heaven, and hell. In our politically correct
climate, none of these subjects is a popular topic for reflection today. Surprisingly, however, many questions are posed
about these articles of the faith from inquirers and Catholics
alike. We do an injustice if we do not give them their proper
attention. Moreover, they are not simply matters for theological argument, but articles of our faith.

From the very beginning of Christianity, belief in the resurrection of the body was attacked as an otherworldly fantasy.
Even Saint Augustine writes: "On no point does the Christian
faith encounter more opposition than on the resurrection of
the body [Footnote: St. Augustine, *En. in Ps.* 88, 5; *PL* 37, 1134]"
(*CCC* 996). It was, at the time of Augustine, much easier to accept the Platonic view, which argued for the immortality of
the soul but dropped all hope in the resurrection of the body.
But Catholic faith teaches both: the immortality of the soul
and the resurrection of the body. Moreover, as the Catechism
affirms: "Belief in the resurrection of the dead has been an
essential element of the Christian faith from its beginnings"
(*CCC* 991). In fact, the yearning to save the body from the rav-
ages of death is as old as human nature itself. The image of
the ancient Egyptians embalming the bodies of the pharaohs
comes immediately to mind.

Importantly, this object of our faith is linked to Jesus' own
resurrection, and it is only in light of his resurrection that we

can understand it correctly as the pattern and cause of our coming resurrection. In fact, Jesus personalizes this belief by saying: "I am the resurrection and the life" (Jn 11:25). It is the hinge, if you will, for this teaching of our faith. Saint Paul makes that quite clear: "If the Spirit of the one who raised Jesus from the dead dwells in you, the one who raised Christ from the dead will give life to your mortal bodies also, through his Spirit that dwells in you" (Rom 8:11).

Despite opposition, the early Christians had confidence and hope in the raising of their bodies. This confidence is again reflected in Saint Paul's First Letter to the Corinthians: "How can some among you say there is no resurrection of the dead? If there is no resurrection of the dead, then neither has Christ been raised. And if Christ has not been raised, then empty [too] is our preaching; empty, too, your faith. . . . But now Christ has been raised from the dead, the firstfruits of those who have fallen asleep" (1 Cor 15:12–14, 20).

The Catechism raises a series of questions, almost apologetic in tone, to help us understand the meaning of the resurrection of the body. What is rising? Answer: In death, the soul lives on and immediately goes to meet God for judgment. The human body decays. The soul awaits the end of time, when God will reunite it with its glorified and resurrected body, which will share either eternal life in heaven or punishment in hell. Who will rise? Answer: All the dead will rise—those who have done good and those who have done bad. How? Answer: We look to Christ—his resurrected body. It was truly Jesus' earthly body, but it was different. He came and went at will. But he did not return to his earthly life. This "how" exceeds our earthly imagination and understanding. It is ultimately accessible only in faith.

Gerald O'Collins and Mary Venturini look to artists and sculptors for some help. Artists go beyond the familiar appearance of the human body to express it in a new way. In doing so they often discover an inner glory in their subjects.

O'Collins and Venturini write: "The resurrection [of the body] can be seen as nothing less than the divine artist disengaging our hidden body of glory." They also describe the transfiguration experience as an example of "luminous and powerful moments from the story of Jesus and some of his saintly followers [that] offer memorable glimpses of what resurrection life could be like." The Catechism compares the resurrection of the body to the Eucharist, calling the Eucharist "a foretaste of Christ's transfiguration of our bodies." It goes on to quote these words of Saint Irenaeus:

> Just as bread that comes from the earth, after God's blessing has been invoked upon it, is no longer ordinary bread, but Eucharist, formed of two things, the one earthly and the other heavenly: so too our bodies, which partake of the Eucharist, are no longer corruptible, but possess the hope of resurrection [Footnote: St. Irenaeus, *Adv. haeres.* 4, 18, 4–5: *PG* 7/1, 1028–1029]. (*CCC* 1000)

Finally, the question: When? Answer: Definitively "at the last day"—at the end of the world. Christ will raise us up on the last day, but in a certain sense, we have already risen with Christ. United with Christ in Baptism, we already truly participate—although in a hidden way—in the heavenly life of the risen Lord, even now.

In expectation of that day when we hope to share fully in Christ's risen life, the Catechism underscores the dignity of belonging even now to the body of Christ. "This dignity entails the demand that [a believer] should treat with respect his own body, but also the body of every other person, especially the suffering" (*CCC* 1004). What does this mean? It "rules out" euthanasia and assisted suicide. It rules in reverence and purity for our bodies and the bodies of others.

To rise means that we must first die. The Catechism speaks of this aspect of the human condition as the one "most shrouded in doubt (*GS* 18)" (*CCC* 1006). Death is the end of earthly life. Death is the consequence of sin. Even though man's nature is mortal, God did not destine human beings to die. Death entered the world as a consequence of sin. Death is the end of our earthly pilgrimage. Finally, death is transformed by Christ. "The obedience of Jesus has transformed the curse of death into a blessing (Cf. Rom 5:19–21)" (*CCC* 1009). It has undone the sin of Adam.

Precisely because of Christ, Christian death has a positive meaning: "If we have died with him / we shall also live with him" (2 Tim 2:11). Or as it is stated in the Preface for the Mass of Christian Burial: "Lord, for your faithful people life is changed, not ended. When the body of our earthly dwelling lies in death we gain an everlasting dwelling place in heaven" (*CCC* 1012).

These are words of *hope*. They are signs of risen life, the life promised us by Jesus. They give meaning to our hope and faith. In the words of Benedict XVI in his 2007 encyclical *Saved by Hope*: "'Hope' in fact, is a key word in Biblical faith—so much so that in several passages the words 'faith' and 'hope' seem interchangeable" (*SS* 2).

At Masses of Christian Burial we seek as best we can to be instruments of consolation and hope for those grieving the loss of a loved one. We are on the lookout for signs of Christian hope.

For the deceased, there is no longer any pain, anxiety, loneliness, or the frailty of the human condition. No longer must the Lord, like the Hound of Heaven, pursue them as he still constantly pursues each one of us in life. As we pray for those who were baptized into Christ Jesus and have now died with him, we remember this wonderful truth of our faith:

> What is essentially new about Christian death is this: through Baptism, the Christian has already "died with Christ" sacramentally, in order to live a new life; and if we die in Christ's grace, physical

> death completes this "dying with Christ" and so completes our incorporation into him in his redeeming act. (CCC 1010)

How easy it is for us to forget in this busy world of ours that we are meant for God. We are created for him and by him. We are meant to go home to our Father's house when our earthly journey is over. Only he knows that moment and that time, for there is "an appointed time for everything." To live with him forever: That after all is the purpose of the end of life. And all of life is a preparation for this final journey. Life is a gift of God, and so, in a mysterious way, is our final breath.

For each of us life is a mystery that only death will ultimately unravel. As we contemplate the lives of those who have fallen asleep in Christ, we are sure that now, at last, in the company of a gracious God, these men and women of faith will finally have the answer to the challenges of their lives fully revealed to them.

Finally, the Catechism teaches that we should nonetheless prepare ourselves for our hour of death. Ask our Blessed Mother in the Hail Mary, for example, to intercede for us "at the hour of our death."

Reflect

1. The one who raised Christ from the dead will give life to your mortal bodies also, through his Spirit that dwells in you (Rom 8:11).

    What do you imagine your resurrected body to be like?

2. This dignity [of the body] entails the demand that [a believer] should treat with respect his own body. . . .

How are you happy or unhappy with the body that God gave you?

3. What else in this chapter was important to you?

Pray

O Lord, our Lord, how awesome is your name
through all the earth!
You have set your majesty above the heavens!
Out of the mouths of babes and infants you have
drawn
a defense against your foes, to silence enemy and
avenger.
When I see your heavens, the work of your
fingers,
the moon and stars that you set in place—
What are humans that you are mindful of them,
mere mortals that you care for them?
Yet you have made them little less than a god,
crowned them with glory and honor.
You have given them rule over the works of your
hands,
put all things at their feet:
All sheep and oxen, even the beasts of the field,
The birds of the air, the fish of the sea,
and whatever swims the paths of the seas.
O Lord, our Lord, how awesome is your name
through all the earth!

   —Psalm 8

TWELVE

And the Life Everlasting

In the *Baltimore Catechism* one of the first questions was: "Why did God make me?" I am sure many of you remember the answer: "God made me to know, love, and serve him in this world and to be happy with him forever in the next." Hence, one of the ends, one of the purposes, of creation is life everlasting. This belief is the last article of the creed: "I believe . . . in life everlasting."

At the heart of our Catholic Tradition is the need for preparation for death, for life everlasting. The best preparation, above all, is a holy life. But there are also the specific sacraments that prepare us for our heavenly homeland. Penance, the Anointing of the Sick, and the Eucharist constitute the three sacraments that complete our earthly pilgrimage. The last Eucharist, called *Viaticum*, "food for the journey," has particular significance. It is the seed of eternal life: "Whoever eats my flesh and drinks my blood has eternal life, and I will raise him on the last day" (Jn 6:54).

When the Church has absolved the dying person from sins, sealed that person with Anointing of the Sick, and given that person *Viaticum*, she speaks with sweet assurance: "Go forth, Christian soul! May your spirit, as it leaves the body, be met by Mary and all the angels and saints. May you see your Redeemer face to face."

Death is followed by judgment. Actually, there are two judgments: the particular judgment (at our death) and the general judgment (at the end of the world). Immediately upon death, the immortal soul faces a "particular judgment."

Each one of us goes immediately at that time to heaven, hell, or purgatory. Each represents a different type of relationship with God.

A Gallup poll concluded that 94 percent of Catholics believe in heaven, while 80 percent believe in hell. Ninety-four percent of Protestants also believe in heaven, and 77 percent believe in hell.

Heaven

Those who die in God's friendship and grace and who are perfectly purified will live forever with Christ. Heaven is not a mailing address beyond the clouds. It is being with Christ forever. ". . . Eye has not seen, and ear has not heard, / and what has not entered the human heart, / what God has prepared for those who love him" (1 Cor 2:9). Heaven is seeing God face to face. This is the beatific vision. It is the perfect life with the Most Blessed Trinity, with the Virgin Mary and all the angels and the saints. It is our ultimate goal and the realization of our deepest desires, a state of supreme and definitive happiness. It is beyond description or imagination. "Scripture uses a variety of pictures to help us understand heaven, such as a wedding party, a banquet, the Father's house, a state of unending happiness" (*USCCA* 154). Artists have taken cues from the Bible to depict heaven as a garden of paradise or a heavenly city or the marriage feast that will never end. We will meet our families and friends again. But, above all, the primary source of our happiness will be communion, union with the tri-personal God made known to us in and through Jesus Christ.

Purgatory

Those who die in God's grace and friendship but who are not fully purified from their sins are assured of eternal salvation. But they must still undergo further purification before entering the heavenly state. It is entirely different from the punishment of the damned. This is purgatory. The Tradition of the Church speaks of "a cleansing fire" or a "purifying fire." Although purgatory has not been spoken of much in recent years, it is still a part of our faith and cannot be ignored.

> The Church assists those in Purgatory through prayer and especially the Eucharist in the their final process of purification. Offering Masses for the deceased is a most powerful way of aiding them. November 2 of each year, the Commemoration of All the Faithful Departed (All Souls Day), is a day for special remembrance and prayer for the dead. (*USCCA* 154)

Hell

"We cannot be united with God unless we freely choose to love him. But we cannot love God if we sin gravely against him, against our neighbor or against ourselves" (CCC 1033). To die in mortal sin without repenting or accepting God's merciful love means remaining separated from him forever by our own free choice. There is an urgency about God's command to love him and neighbor. This state of definitive self-exclusion from communion with God and the blessed is called hell. It is the ultimate punishment for failure to love God, neighbor, and ourselves. It is eternal separation from God. The teaching of the Church affirms the existence of hell and the possibility of ending up there. Fear and guilt are not the proper responses to the reality of hell. To face the possibility of hell honestly and maturely is to accept the daily call to responsibility and the urgent call to daily conversion. "Enter through the narrow gate; for the gate is wide and the road is broad that leads to destruction, and those who enter through it are many. How narrow the gate and constricted the road that leads to life. And those who find it are few" (Mt 7:13–14).

In addition to speaking of heaven, hell, and purgatory, the Church has in the past spoken of limbo. It traditionally has been seen as the fate at death of unbaptized infants who through no fault of their own were not baptized. The "theory" of limbo has attempted to deal with souls of infants who die subject to original sin and without Baptism and who therefore neither merit the beatific vision nor yet are subjected to any punishment because they are not guilty of any personal sin, i.e., a state where unbaptized infants spend eternity without communion with God.

On January 19, 2007, the International Theological Commission issued its study of the "theory" of limbo. It held that this theory is not even mentioned in the Catechism because it has no clear foundation in revelation and reflects "an unduly restrictive view of salvation."

Because of original sin, Baptism is certainly the ordinary way to salvation, and parents are urged to baptize their children as soon as they can. At the same time, the commission concluded that there are reasons for prayerful hope that unbaptized infants who die will be saved and enjoy the beatific vision. The Church's hope for these infants' salvation reflects a growing awareness of God's mercy.

Earlier in this section, I spoke of the particular judgment that each of us receives at the moment of death. The final or last judgment takes place at the end of the world. "The holy Roman Church firmly believes and confesses that on the Day of Judgment all men will appear in their own bodies before Christ's tribunal to render an account of their own deeds [Footnote: Council of Lyons II (1274): DS 859; cf. DS 1549]" (CCC 1059). This will be the resurrection of all the dead, "the righteous and the unrighteous" (Acts 24:15). In the presence of Christ, the truth of each person's relationship with God will be laid bare.

When I visit Rome I often visit the Sistine Chapel to view Michelangelo's newly refurbished fresco of the Last Judgment. I cannot help hearing the words of Matthew's Gospel resonating in my ears as I look each time at this magnificent piece of art: "When the Son of Man comes in his glory, and all the angels with him . . . all the nations will be assembled before him. And he will separate them one from another, as a shepherd separates the sheep from the goats. He will place the sheep on his right and the goats on his left. . . . [The goats] will go off to eternal punishment, but the righteous to eternal life" (Mt 25:31–33, 46).

In his book *Essentials of the Faith: A Guide to the Catechism of the Catholic Church*, Fr. Alfred McBride recounts a legend about the Sistine Chapel fresco of the Last Judgment. It claims that a cardinal disliked the artist's use of nudity and harassed Michelangelo about it. Irritated, Michelangelo put him in the fresco, writhing in hell. Outraged, the cardinal reportedly said to the pope: "Make him take me out of there." Amused, the pope replied: "Eminence, you know very well that I can only help people get out of purgatory." The fresco is quite overwhelming—the fires of hell, the gray faces of those there, this cardinal wrapped in a serpent. One could not help but pause.

The thought of the Last Judgment should not riddle us or paralyze us, however, with worldly fear, but in the words of the Catechism, "it inspires a holy fear of God." It should call us to a deeper conversion. "It proclaims the 'blessed hope' of the Lord's return, when he will come 'to be glorified in his saints, and to be marveled at in all who have believed' (Titus 2:13; 2 Thess 1:10)" (*CCC* 1041). In *Saved by Hope*, Pope Benedict gives us further encouragement about the Last Judgment when he writes: "The incarnation of God in Christ has so closely linked the two together—judgment and grace—that justice is firmly established: we all work out our salvation 'with fear and trembling' (Phil 2:12). Nevertheless grace allows us all to hope, and to go trustfully to meet the Judge whom we know as our 'advocate' . . ." (*SS* 47).

We know not when the end of the world will come. But when it does, the kingdom of God will come in its fullness. We live in the hope of "a new heaven and a new earth" (Rev 21:1). The just will reign with Christ forever, in body and soul, and the material world will also be transformed. God will then be "all in all" (1 Cor 15:28) in eternal life.

In the words of then-Cardinal Ratzinger: "You, Lord, are yourself the new heaven, the heaven in which God is a man. Give us the new earth in which we men become branches of you, the tree of life, steeped in the waters of your love and taken up into the ascent to the Father, who alone is the true progress we all await."

Amen.

At the end of the Creed, we say "Amen." It is another way of saying "I believe." In Hebrew, *Amen* comes from the same root as the word for "to believe." But as we say "Amen" to this reflection on the Apostles' Creed and the first pillar of the Catechism, let us not cease in our pursuit of deeper understanding and acceptance of the faith we profess. I suggest we follow the advice of the then-Cardinal Ratzinger in the introduction to a book he coauthored with Cardinal Christoph Schönborn on the Catechism:

> Thanks to the sizable number of cross-references, but also to the citations of the Fathers and saints, whoever takes the time to become acquainted with this first and longest part of the catechism will be able to ascertain to what a degree statements about the faith are intimately connected with the entire Christian life, which finds expression in the celebration of the liturgy, in prayer and in moral action. Numerous testimonies of holy

men and women prove how deeply faith can penetrate one's life in order to transform it into a new
life in Christ. The words of Saint Augustine at the
close of the first part are a stimulus to such con-
templative reading: "May your Creed be for you
as a mirror. Look at yourself in it, to see if you believe everything you say you believe. And rejoice
in your faith each day." (CCC 1064)

Let our "Amen" resound in unity with that of Jesus, who
is the definitive "Amen" to the Father's love for us. He takes
up and completes our "Amen" to the Father: "For all the
promises of God find their Yes in him. That is why we ut-
ter the Amen through him, to the glory of God (2 Cor 1:20)"
(CCC 1065).

Reflect

1. Eye has not seen, and ear has not heard, / and what
   has not entered the human heart, / what God has
   prepared for those who love him (1 Cor 2:9).

   How do you imagine heaven?

2. All who die in God's grace and friendship, but still
   imperfectly purified, are indeed assured of their
   eternal salvation; but after death they undergo
   purification, so as to achieve the holiness necessary to
   enter the joy of heaven (CCC 1030).

   How do you imagine purgatory?

3. This state of definitive self-exclusion from
   communion with God and the blessed is called "hell"
   (CCC 1033).

How do you imagine hell?

4. How do these images shape your everyday life of
   faith?

5. What else in this chapter was important to you?

Pray

Choose Life

Blessed be your name, Lord God,
who has set before me life and death,
and has invited me to choose life.
Now, Lord God, I choose life, with all my heart.
I choose you, my God, for you are my life.
Lord, make me completely holy,
that all my spirit, soul and body
may be a temple for you.
Live in me, and be my God
and I will be your servant.

—Thomas Ken

Abbreviations

CCC Catechism of the Catholic Church. Vatican
City: Liberia Editrice Vaticana, Second Edition, 1997. (The references in the text are to
paragraph numbers.)

*USCCA United States Catholic Catechism for
Adults.* Washington, D.C.: U.S. Conference of
Catholic Bishops Publishing, 2006. (The ref-
erences in the text are to page numbers.)

*AG Decree on the Church's Missionary Activity (Ad
Gentes Divinitus).* Vatican Council II, 1965.

*CD Decree Concerning the Pastoral Office of Bishops
(Christus Dominus).* Paul VI, 1965.

CDF Congregation for the Doctrine of the Faith.

CPG Credo of the People of God

*CT On Catechesis in Our Time (Catechesi Traden-
dae).* Apostolic Exhortation of Pope John Paul
II, 1979.

*DEV The Lord and Giver of Life (Dominum et Vivi-
ficantem).* Encyclical of Pope John Paul II,
1986.

*DM On the Dignity and Vocation of Women (Mu-
lieris Dignitatem).* Apostolic Letter of Pope
John Paul II, 1988.

*DS Denzinger-Schönmetzer, Enchiridion Symbolo-
rum, definitionum et declarationum de rebus fidei
et morum, 1965.*

DV *Dogmatic Constitution on Divine Revelation (Dei Verbum).* Vatican Council II, 1965.

FR *Faith and Reason (Fides et Ratio),* Encyclical of Pope John Paul II, 1998.

GS *The Church in the Modern World (Gaudium et Spes),* Vatican Council II, 1965.

ID *Doctrine on Indulgences (Indulgentiarum Doctrina)* Apostolic Constitution of Pope Paul VI, 1967.

LG *Dogmatic Constitution on the Church (Lumen Gentium).* Vatican Council II, 1966.

PG J.P. Migne, ed., *Patroligia Greaca* (Paris, 1867-1866).

PL J.P. Migne, ed., *Patroligia Latina* (Paris, 1841-1855).

SC *The Sacrament of Clarity (Sacramentum Caritatis).* Post-Synodal Apostolic Exhortation of Pope Benedict XVI, 2007.

SD *On the Christian Meaning of Human Suffering (Salvifici Doloris).* Apostolic Letter of Pope John Paul II, 1984.

SS *Saved by Hope (Spe Salvi).* Encyclical of Pope Benedict XVI, 2007.

UUS *On Commitment to Ecumenism (Ut Unum Sint).* Encyclical Letter of John Paul II, 1995.

VS *The Splendor of Truth (Veritatis Splendor).* Encyclical of Pope John Paul II, 1993.

The papal and conciliar documents cited above can be found on the Vatican website: www.vatican.va. Use the Latin name when searching for them. Quotations and homilies by the pope can also be found on the Vatican website. Search by the date of the address.

References

Prologue

A transcript of Pope Benedict's interview with German television can be found at: www.freerepublic.com/focus/f-religion/1684006/posts

John Paul II, Homily on World Communications Day, May 16, 1990.

"The Hound of Heaven" was written by Francis Thompson sometime before his death in 1907. The poem became famous and was the source of much of Thompson's posthumous reputation. It was included in the *Oxford Book of Mystical Verse* published in 1917.

Chapter 1

Walter Kasper, *The God of Jesus Christ* (New York: The Crossroad Publishing Company, 1986), p. 296.

Gerald O'Collins, S.J., and Mary Venturini, *Believing: Understanding the Creed* (London: T. & T. Clark Publishers, 1996), pp. 33–34.

Ibid., p. 45.

The description of Mont-Saint-Michel is from Robert G. Calkins, "Carnival on a Rock," *The Wall Street Journal*, October 7–8, 2006.

A new edition of Henry Adams's *Mont-Saint-Michel and Chartres* was published by Kessinger Publishing in 2005.

The *Time* magazine cover story on angels appeared in the December 27, 1993, issue, pp. 56 ff.

Christoph Schönborn, O.P., *Living the Catechism of the Catholic Church* (San Francisco: Ignatius Press, 1995), p. 52.

John Paul II, *Crossing the Threshold of Hope* (New York: Knopf, 1994), pp. 57–58.

Chapter 2

The poem "One Solitary Life" is often attributed as anonymous but is probably the work of Rev. James Allan Francis. Its earliest publication is in a book by Aldridge, *The Real Jesus and Other Sermons*, published in 1926 by Judson Press in Philadelphia (cf. pp. 123–124 , "Arise Sir Knight!").

O'Collins and Venturini, p. 55.

Chapter 3

Joseph Ratzinger and Christoph von Schönborn, O.P., *An Introduction to the Catechism of the Catholic Church* (San Francisco: Ignatius Press, 1994), p. 72.

Cardinal O'Connor's homily appeared in *Catholic New York*, p. 14, January 20, 1994.

Chapter 4

Donald Wuerl, Thomas Comerford Lawler, Ronald Lawler, eds., *The Gift of Faith: A Question and Answer Catechism Version of the Teaching of Christ* (Huntington, IN: Our Sunday Visitor, 1981), p. 79.

O'Collins and Venturini, pp. 79–80.

Wuerl, Lawler, and Lawler, p. 77.

Chapter 5

Walter Burghardt, *Grace on Crutches* (Mahwah, NJ: Paulist Press, 1986), p. 30.

O'Collins and Venturini, p. 100.

O'Collins and Venturini, pp. 102–103.

Chapter 6

"Justice in the World," World Synod of Bishops, 1971, par. 6.

Augustine's words are found in the second reading in the Office of Readings for the Feast of the Ascension.

Chapter 7

O'Collins and Venturini, p. 124.

Chapter 11

O'Collins and Venturini, pp. 165, 168.

Chapter 12

Alfred McBride, *Essentials of the Faith: A Guide to the Catechism of the Catholic Church* (Huntington, IN: Our Sunday Visitor, 2002), p. 108.

Joseph Ratzinger, *Images of Hope: Meditations on Major Feasts* (San Francisco: Ignatius Press, 2006), p. 78.

Joseph Ratzinger and Christoph Schönborn, O.P., pp. 79–80.

Msgr. Peter J. Vaghi is pastor of the Church of the Little Flower in Bethesda, Maryland, and a priest of the Archdiocese of Washington. Prior to his seminary studies at the North American College and the Gregorian University in Rome, he practiced law. He remains a member of the Virginia State Bar and the District of Columbia Bar, and is chaplain of the John Carroll Society, a group of professionals and businesspersons in service of the Archbishop of Washington. He has written a number of articles for *America* and *Priest* magazines and for *Our Sunday Visitor* newspaper. He is also a contributor to *Behold Your Mother: Priests Speak about Mary* (Ave Maria Press).

Know Your Faith

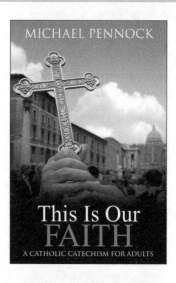

This Is Our Faith
A Catholic Catechism for Adults
Michael Pennock
This popular Catholic faith primer for adults corresponds with the four pillars of the Catechism and includes discussion questions and prayer exercises.
ISBN: 9780877936534 / 368 pages / $14.95

Also Available:
Questions of Faith
*A Workbook Companion to
the Catechism of the Catholic Church*
ISBN: 9780877936893 / 96 pages / $6.95

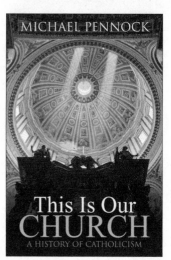

This Is Our Church
A History of Catholicism
Michael Pennock
A historical narrative of the Church, this resource provides an in-depth historical approach to church history, revealing the rich and varied stories that help form the Catholic identity.
ISBN: 9781594710759 / 360 pages, w/ 8-page color insert / $21.95